Easy PCs,
Fourth Edition

Suzanne Weixel

Easy PCs, Fourth Edition

International Standard Book Number: 0-7897-0455-2

Library of Congress Catalog Card Number: 95-71045

98   8 7 6 5 4 2

Interpretation of the printing code: the rightmost double-digit number is the year of the book's first printing; the rightmost single-digit number is the number of the book's printing. For example, a printing code of 95-1 shows that this copy of the book was printed during the first printing of the book in 1995.

This book was produced digitally by Macmillan Computer Publishing and manufactured using computer-to-plate technology (a film-less process) by GAC/Shepard Poorman, Indianapolis, Indiana.

Dedication

It's still for Nathaniel and Evan.

Credits

Publisher
Roland Elgey

Vice-President and Publisher
Marie Butler-Knight

Publishing Manager
Barry Pruett

Director of Editorial Services
Elizabeth Keaffaber

Managing Editor
Michael Cunningham

Development Editors
Lori Cates
David Bradford

Senior Editor
Michelle Shaw

Copy Editors
Rebecca Mayfield
Tom Certin
Dianna Evans

Designer
Barb Kordesh

Cover Designer
Dan Armstrong
Kim Scott

Technical Specialist
Cari Skaggs

Indexer
Mary Jane Frisby

Production Team
Claudia Bell, Jason Carr, Amy Cornwell,
Anne Dickerson, Jason Hand, Mike
Henry, John Hulse, Daryl Kessler, Clint
Lahnen, Bob LaRoche, Gina Rexrode,
Claire Schweinler, Scott Tullis, Kelly
Warner, Jody York

*Special thanks to Marty Wyatt for ensuring
the technical accuracy of this book.*

Composed in *Stone Serif* and *MCPdigital* by Que Corporation

About the Author

Suzanne Weixel is a self-employed writer and editor specializing in the technology industry. Her experience with computers began in 1974 when she learned to play football on the Dartmouth Time Sharing terminal her brother installed in a spare bedroom. For Que, Suzanne has written and revised numerous books, including *Easy PCs*, 3rd Edition, *Word 6 for Windows QuickStart*, *I Hate Word 6 for Windows*, *Ami Pro 3 QuickStart*, *DOS 6 QuickStart*, *Everyday DOS*, *Using Windows 3.11*, and *Using DOS*. She also writes about non-computer-related subjects whenever she has the chance.

Suzanne graduated from Dartmouth College in 1981 with a degree in art history. She currently lives in Marlborough, MA with her husband; their sons, Nathaniel and Evan; and their Samoyed, Cirrus.

Acknowledgments

Thanks to the editorial and production staffs at Que for all their hard work.

Trademark Acknowledgments

All terms mentioned in this book that are known to be trademarks or service marks have been appropriately capitalized. Que Corporation cannot attest to the accuracy or this information. Use of a term in this book should not be regarded as affecting the validity of any trademark or service mark.

Contents

Part IV: Understanding Common PC Components   67

Part V: Understanding Your Operating System   91

Part VI: Windows 95 Tasks   107

Part VII: DOS Tasks   155

Part VIII: Using Your Computer   177

Glossary   204

Index   220

Introduction

It's easy to be intimidated by computers. You hear words like *chip* and *processor*, and acronyms like *VGA* and *RAM*, and may decide that being computer-ignorant is easier than being computer-literate. However, much of the learning about a PC is seeing the machine for what it is—a tool you can use to get ahead in your job, keep your household more organized, write letters, or just have fun.

How You Can Use a PC

Here are just a few of the tasks you can perform with a PC:

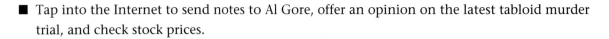

- Use a word processing program to write letters, memos, or the Great American Novel.

- Balance your checkbook with a personal finance or *spreadsheet* program.

- Store recipes, addresses, and telephone numbers using a database program.

- Tap into the Internet to send notes to Al Gore, offer an opinion on the latest tabloid murder trial, and check stock prices.

- Issue a newsletter using a desktop publishing program.

- Teach your kids math (or any other subject) using one of zillions of educational programs.

- Pretend you are flying a Stealth Bomber using a flight simulator program.

- Look up any topic in a CD-ROM–based encyclopedia.

- Create presentations that combine live-action video, animation, sound, and graphics.

This book shows you the magic behind the computer screen. It teaches you how to understand computers and how to take control of the great technology on your desktop.

How This Book Is Organized

This book is designed so that you can find all the information you need, without having to flip through a lot of pages. You don't need to be a computer guru to understand anything presented in this book. Pictures and diagrams present the information, while straightforward text and clear-cut definitions provide explanations you can understand at a glance.

The book is divided into nine parts. Each part contains sections that completely explore specific topics, all on a few pages.

In Part I, "Understanding Computer Basics," you learn to identify the basic components found in nearly all personal computers, and to understand what each piece is used for.

In Part II, "Getting Started," you learn how to set up, start, and care for your PC and its software.

In Part III, "Understanding What Makes Your Computer Work," you learn what goes on inside your computer. You'll discover what really controls the computer processing, the amount of memory your computer needs, and how disk drives work.

In Part IV, "Getting to Know Your Computer," you learn more about the basic PC components and how they work. In this part, you find out what makes a multimedia computer different, how being on a network affects your work, and how to use communications applications.

In Part V, "Understanding Your Operating System," you learn about the software that makes your PC work, and how to use it. You also get an overview of Windows 95, the latest operating system from Microsoft.

In Part VI, "Windows Tasks," step-by-step instructions lead you through several series of tasks, designed to teach you how to use the Windows 95 operating system. Among other things, you learn how to start programs, find out what is on a disk, and control windows.

In Part VII, "DOS Tasks," you learn some useful DOS commands by following step-by-step instructions that knock DOS down to size.

In Part VIII, "Using Your Computer," you learn about the different kinds of programs you can use to accomplish specific tasks with your PC, and you learn how to decide which programs you need. You also learn about today's hottest new technologies: multimedia and the Internet.

Finally, there is a glossary that defines frequently used terms.

You can read the book from start to finish, or you can jump around to look for the topics you need.

How to Use the Task Sections

The Task sections consist of numbered steps that teach you how to accomplish certain things, such as copying a file or resizing a window. The numbered steps walk you through a specific example so that you can learn the task by actually doing it.

Big Screen

At the beginning of each task is a large picture of your PC screen showing the results of the task, or some other key element of the task, such as a shortcut menu.

TASK 13

Changing Disks and Directories

C:\WINDOWS>cd\

C:\>

"Why would I do this?"

Each task includes a brief explanation of how you benefit from knowing how to accomplish the task.

"Why would I do this?"

DOS executes most commands on the current drive in the current directory (or folder). Although you can add parameters to the command to specify a different file or directory, it's usually easier to make the different drive or directory current. Then you just type the command without additional parameters.

In this task, you learn how to change to a different disk and to the root directory. Before you begin this task, insert a formatted disk into drive A.

C:\WINDOWS>cd\

C:\>

158

Step-by-Step Screens

Each step in each task is illustrated with a picture of what should appear on your PC screen as you perform that step.

Task 13: Changing Disks and Directories

1 At the DOS prompt, type A: and press **Enter**. A: is the name of the drive you want to make current. DOS switches to drive A and displays the name of the current drive (now A) in the DOS prompt (usually as A:\>). To change drives, you type the name of the drive and press **Enter**.

NOTE

The name of a disk drive is a letter followed by a colon (:), so A: is the name of floppy disk drive A, and C: is the name of hard drive C.

2 At the DOS prompt, type C: and press **Enter** to change back to drive C.

WHY WORRY?

If you see the message, Not ready reading drive A Abort, Retry, Fail? it means that there is no disk in the drive, or that you inserted the disk incorrectly. Put a formatted disk in the drive, and press R to try again.

If you see the message General failure reading drive A Abort, Retry, Fail?, it means that the disk you inserted in the drive is not formatted. Insert a formatted disk, and press R to try again.

3 At the DOS prompt, type CD\ and press **Enter**. CD is the command that tells DOS to change directories, and \ is the symbol for the root directory. DOS changes to the root directory. DOS displays the name of the current directory (in this case, the root) in the DOS prompt. To change to a directory, use the CD command followed by the directory name. From there, you can progress to subdirectories within the current directory by typing **CD** and the subdirectory name ■

159

Other Notes

Many tasks include short notes that tell you a little more about certain procedures. For example, these notes may define terms, explain other options, refer you to other sections, or provide hints and shortcuts.

Why Worry? Notes

The Why Worry? notes tell you how to undo certain procedures, or how to get out of an unexpected situation.

5

Where to Get More Help

As you become more comfortable with a computer, you may need a more complete reference book. Que offers several books to suit your needs.

If you still need to know more about PCs before progressing to books on specific topics, these are good books to have:

- *Using Your PC*

- *Que's Computer User's Dictionary*

- *Computers: A Visual Encyclopedia*

- *Complete Idiot's Guide to Upgrading Your PC*

If you have a handle on basic PC concepts and want to learn more about the DOS operating system, try these books:

- *Easy DOS, Version 6.2*

- *Complete Idiot's Guide to DOS*

- *Using DOS*

If you want to learn more about using Windows 95, the latest operating system from Microsoft, you'll want to read one of these books:

- *Easy Windows 95*

- *Complete Idiot's Guide to Windows 95*

- *Using Windows 95*

If you have a computer whose operating system was installed before 1995, you probably have Windows 3.1 (or Windows 3.11) and will want to read these books:

- *Easy Windows 3.11*

- *Complete Idiot's Guide to Windows*

- *Using Windows 3.11*

PART I

Understanding Computer Basics

What Is a Computer?

Believe it or not, a computer is just an appliance—a machine built from plastic and metal, designed to automate routine tasks. Some appliances, such as toaster ovens and vacuum cleaners, relieve the tedium of everyday chores. Some appliances, like televisions and CD players, add enjoyment to everyday life. Computers do both.

Of course, a computer is a bit more complicated than a toaster oven, but that's what makes it interesting and fun. With a toaster oven, you can bake, broil, or toast. With a computer, you can organize, calculate, design, educate, schedule, illustrate, edit, communicate... the list is nearly endless!

Inside all appliances are wires and cables and nuts and bolts that you probably will never see, let alone touch. The same is true for computers, but the more you know, the better off you are when it comes to buying new equipment or getting old equipment repaired. Or for the curious, knowing how it all works.

What Is Hardware?

The physical parts of the computer—the parts that you can see and touch—are called *hardware*. The keyboard, the monitor, and the box that houses the guts of the computer—the system unit—are all hardware. So are the cables that connect them, the electronics that make them work, and the screws that hold them together.

Computer hardware also includes other machines attached to the computer, called *peripherals*. Some peripherals that you may have include printers, modems, and mice.

What Is Software?

Software refers to the programs that you run on a computer. The programs are made up of coded instructions that tell the hardware how to process information. There are two types of software programs:

■ System software determines how the different pieces of hardware will operate, and how the PC responds to commands. Some people like to think of system software as the traffic cop that controls and coordinates the flow of information within the computer system. MS-DOS (which stands for *Microsoft Disk Operating System*), NetWare, Windows, UNIX, and OS/2 are examples of common system software programs. System software is usually built into the computer, or installed on your computer by someone else, either before you buy the computer, or when it is attached to other computers. By the way—when your computer is attached to other computers, it's part of a *network*. You'll learn more about networks in the section called, "What You Need to Know About Networks," in Part IV, "Getting to Know Your Computer."

A (Brief) History of Personal Computers

The earliest computers were impractical. They filled entire rooms, cost a small fortune, and were incapable of performing many useful functions. Like a brontosaurus—big and bulky, and not too bright—they were more suited to science fiction than to homes and businesses.

The promise was there, however, and researchers worked hard to find ways to fit more and more processing power into smaller and smaller boxes. In 1981, IBM introduced a *microcomputer*—a machine designed to fit on a desktop and provide information processing for one person—and called it the IBM Personal Computer (PC).

The IBM PC is no longer the only microcomputer on the block. Other manufacturers make PCs that are *compatible* with the IBM PC. Compatible means that the computers are based on the same technology as the IBM machines, and can run the same programs. Compatibles are referred to as clones, because they are built to perform the same as the IBM products.

Some manufacturers have developed personal computers that use completely different technology. These computers, such as Apple's Macintosh series, are not generally compatible with IBM PCs, and although they are personal computers, they are not usually referred to as PCs. That's not to say they are not as good—just different. You have to decide which type is better for you.

All PCs require hardware and software in order to work. Hardware provides the foundation, and software provides the information. You can think of the software as the brains and the hardware as the brawn.

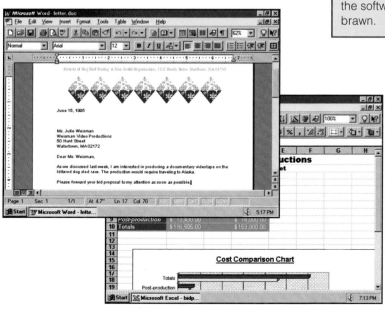

■ Application software is used to perform specific tasks such as word processing and desktop publishing. Lotus 1-2-3 and WordPerfect are two common application programs. You install applications using floppy disks, CD-ROMs, or by transferring them from other computers attached to the same network as your computer.

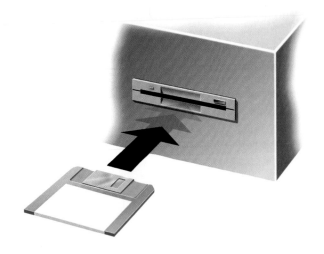

Basic Hardware Components

Most PCs sold today are built around the same basic hardware components.

With the earliest PCs, you could get only the necessary hardware components packaged in one basic model. Now, advancements in technology have made it possible to package these same basic components in different ways. As long as you have the basic system components, the size and shape of a PC are a matter of personal preference or necessity.

System Unit

The system unit is the box, or case, that contains the "guts" of your PC. If you took the top off the box, you would see the electrical components—the electronic chips, wires, and circuits—that actually do the information processing.

> **NOTE** ▼
>
> The concept of "software" can be difficult to grasp because you cannot actually see or touch the codes that make up the software instructions, but without software, your PC would be virtually useless. Try thinking of software like a videotape and a computer like a VCR. The PC plays the software the way a VCR plays the tape. It is software that tells your PC everything from how to respond when you press the Shift key on your keyboard, to whether to act as a word processor, or as a graphic designer.

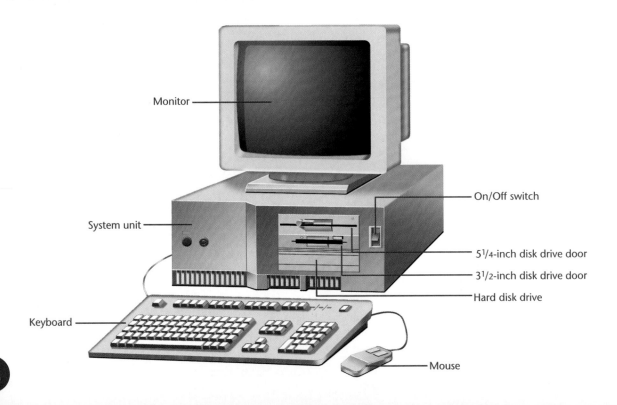

Monitor

System unit

Keyboard

On/Off switch

5¹/₄-inch disk drive door

3¹/₂-inch disk drive door

Hard disk drive

Mouse

The computer's *on/off switch* is located on the system unit. The *main power cord* is attached to the system unit. *Indicator lights* on the front of the system unit show you which options are turned on, such as what mode of operation is being used and whether the power is on.

> **NOTE** ▼
>
> You probably will never need to open the system unit, but if you do, be very careful. It takes only a tiny amount of dirt, disruption or static electricity from your fingers to damage the components inside the box, but it may take a considerable amount of time and money to repair them.

Most system units also have a reset button so that you can restart the computer without shutting it off, and a turbo button that lets you run the PC at a faster speed. Be careful that you do not press the reset button accidentally. You might damage your software programs or lose the information you are working with.

Inside the system unit, you find the most important piece of the computer, the *central processing unit* (CPU), as well as the computer's memory.

> **NOTE** ▼
>
> Be careful that you do not press the reset button accidentally. You might damage your software or lose the information you are working on.

All peripherals are attached to the system unit. Some peripherals, such as internal modem cards, fit into sockets inside the box, called *slots*. Other peripherals, such as printers, are attached with cables to sockets, called *ports*, on the outside of the system unit.

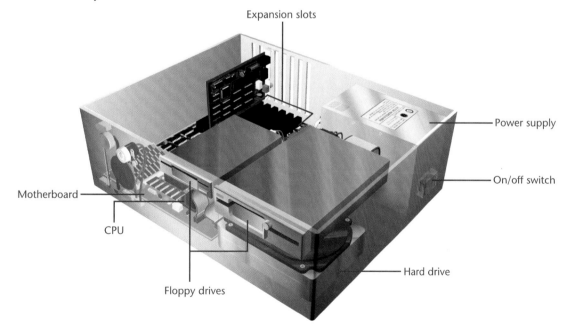

Expansion slots

Power supply

On/off switch

Motherboard

CPU

Hard drive

Floppy drives

For more detailed information on what is inside the system unit, see Part III, "Understanding What Makes Your Computer Work."

Display screen

Controls   On/off switch

The Monitor

The *monitor*, also called the screen or the display, shows both the information you type on the keyboard and the computer's response to this information. When you press a key on the keyboard, for example, the typed letter appears on the monitor. When you type a command, you see the computer's response to the command.

Monitors can be *monochrome*, which means that you see one color at a time on the background, while color monitors allow you to display a range of colors. Like a TV, most monitors have an on/off switch and knobs to control brightness and contrast. For more information, see the section "Understanding Monitors" in Part IV, "Getting to Know Your Computer."

The Keyboard

You use the *keyboard* to input information into the computer. The keyboard has all the keys that a typewriter keyboard has, plus some keys unique to computers. For example, your keyboard probably has *special-purpose keys*, such as Ctrl (Control) and Alt (Alternate) keys. With these keys, you input commands specific to the software you are using. Likewise, in most application programs, if the information you are looking at does not all fit on-screen at the same time, press the key labeled PgDn (Page Down). The monitor displays the next screen of information. Try doing this on a typewriter!

Function keys   Indicator lights

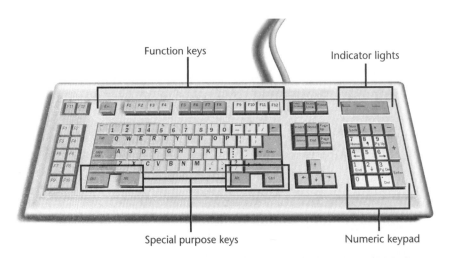

Special purpose keys   Numeric keypad

You can choose from a wide variety of keyboard styles, depending on the PC you have or the applications you usually use. Most laptop-sized portable PC keyboards, for example, are smaller than desktop PC keyboards, but even desktop PCs can have different keyboards. For more information, see the section "Understanding Keyboards" in Part IV, "Getting to Know Your Computer."

The Mouse

You can use the *mouse*—a small, hand-held pointing device—instead of, or in conjunction with, a keyboard to input commands. For example, a mouse provides a useful way to select menu options in Microsoft Windows. For more information, see the section "Understanding Mice" in Part IV, "Getting To Know Your Computer."

The Disk Drives

Disk drives are devices that the computer uses to store information that is not currently in use. Disk drives hold disks that the computer can read information from, and—except for CD-ROM drives—write information to. Disk drives are

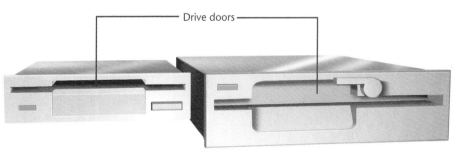

Drive doors

similar to phonographs or CD players—the disk rotates inside the drive as an arm moves across the disk and a head on the end of the arm interprets electrical signals between the computer and the disk.

The different types of disk drives include floppy drives, hard drives, and CD-ROM drives. For more information about disk drives, see the section, "Understanding Data Storage" in Part III, "What Makes Your Computer Work."

Floppy Drives

Floppy disk drives are usually built into the system unit. You insert and remove floppy disks via disk drive doors, which look like mail slots in the box. Floppy disks are used to install application programs, store information, and read stored information.

Hard Drives

Hard disk drives are either built into the system unit or attached to it via cables. Because most hard disks cannot be removed, they are sometimes called *fixed disks.*

> **NOTE** ▼
>
> Most disk drives have in-use lights on the front of the system unit. When the PC is reading or writing information to a disk in that drive, the light is on. You should never open a drive door, eject a disk, or turn off the computer when a drive in-use light is on.

Hard disks can hold far more information than floppy disks, and they are not as easily damaged. Before hard disks were available, people spent much of their time inserting and removing floppy disks and waiting while the computer either read the information from, or wrote information onto, the floppy. Hard disks made PCs much easier and faster to use. Most PCs sold today have at least one internal hard disk.

CD-ROM Drives

CD-ROM drives, like hard disk drives, are built into the system unit or attached to it via cables. CD-ROM stands for compact disk, read-only memory. It's pronounced as if it were three separate words. See-Dee-ROM. CD-ROM drives are used to read information from compact disks, just like the CD player you may have in your home or in your car. In fact, the CD-ROM drive in your computer can probably play your music CDs, as well as your computer CDs (but don't try to play your computer CDs in your CD player—it doesn't work and may damage the equipment).

CD-ROMs can hold even more information than hard disks, but, although your computer can read data off a CD-ROM, it cannot write data onto one. CD-ROMs are used mostly for multimedia applications, such as displaying animation and video on your computer screen and playing sound. CD-ROMs are also often used for installing application programs. For more information about CD-ROMs and multimedia, see "What Is a Multimedia Computer" in Part IV, "Getting to Know Your Computer?"

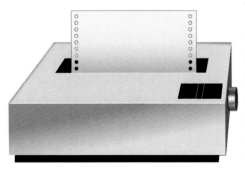

The Printer

You use a *printer* to print copies of the computer data. After you see the information on the monitor, you can print the data for other uses. The printed material is often called *hard copy*, to differentiate it from the data stored on a disk or held in the computer's memory. For more information, see the section called "Understanding Printers" in Part IV, "Getting to Know Your Computer."

The Modem

You use a *modem* to connect the computer to a telephone line. You can use the modem to call other computers and to exchange information with them. For example, a modem lets you connect with an online service company such as CompuServe that lets you get information from other computers, download files from the Internet, and send electronic mail to your uncle in Wichita. Some modems have built-in fax capabilities that enable you to connect with facsimile machines. For more information, see the section called "What You Need to Know About Communications" in Part IV, "Getting to Know Your Computer."

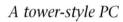

Types of Computers

The traditional PC is called a *desktop model* because it fits nicely on most desks and is suitable for most people to use at work or at home. Some desktop models have a *small footprint* case, which means the case is designed to take up less space. Small footprint models usually stand higher than other desktop models, so that they still have room inside for the same basic components, despite the shorter length and width.

There are two other common variations on the basic PC system:

A tower-style PC

- A *tower model* looks like a desktop model standing on its side. Tower PCs can stand on the floor under the desk, leaving your desktop free and providing easy access to controls such as the on/off switch, as well as to the interior components. Tower models are larger than desktop models and have more room inside for future growth. They also usually cost more than desktop models.

- A *portable PC* is one that is small enough to be easily carried along when you need to work away from your desk. All the basic components are built into the unit, not attached with cables. Most portables have no room for future growth, although some can be attached to external peripherals such as disk drives, and even to so-called docking units, which transform the portable into a desktop model.

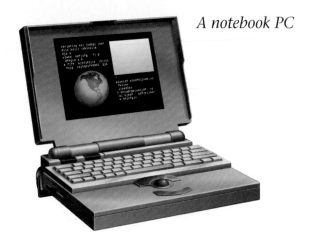

A notebook PC

Portables are classified by weight, ranging from laptops (8 to 10 pounds) to notebooks (6 to 8 pounds) to subnotebooks (2 to 6 pounds). Although portables are more convenient than desktop models, they are usually not as easy to use—because these computers are so small, the basic components such as the keyboard and the display screen also must be small.

Keep these guidelines in mind when deciding which type of computer style you are going to buy:

■ If you do most of your computing at your desk, and you don't plan to add many peripherals or memory, you can buy a basic desktop PC.

■ If you need to access information or draft memos while flying home from a sales call, you can buy a portable PC that fits in a briefcase.

■ If you need more space on your desktop, or you plan to attach lots of peripherals to the PC, you can buy a tower model.

How Computers Work

Like most appliances, computers run on electricity and plug right into the outlets in your home or office, or—in the case of portables—have batteries. After you plug in your computer and turn it on, its electronic circuitry is ready to go. All it needs is your command. From input to output, getting results from a computer is accomplished in three basic steps:

1 **You enter data.** You can enter data (information such as words or numbers) using any input device, such as the keyboard or a mouse, or from files stored on disks. Some computers even recognize spoken words.

2 **The computer processes the data.** The computer translates the data into electrical signals that it can process by using its memory, the CPU, and circuitry. The way the computer processes the signals depends on the software program you are using. Different programs contain different instructions. For example, a word processing program contains instructions about which key controls inserting or overwriting text. A spreadsheet program contains instructions for performing calculations. The computer interprets the instructions and performs the required task.

3 **The computer outputs the result as new data.** The electrical signals are then sent to an output device, which translates the signals back into a format that you can understand. For example, the data may appear on the screen, print on a printer, or be saved on a disk for storage. Sometimes output is simply held in the computer's memory until you need it.

NOTE ▼

Data is any kind of information you can imagine. Most commonly, we use PCs to process data in the form of words, numbers, or pictures, but they can also be used to process sounds and video.

PART II
Getting Started

Setting Up the Work Area

When you take home a new appliance, you need to set it up before you use it. For example, if you bring home a new stereo or CD player, you have to find a place for it, attach the receiver, hook up and position the speakers, and finally plug it in the appropriate outlet. The same is true for a computer.

You should give some thought to what constitutes a good work area. If you are setting up the PC at your office, you are probably limited to your current desk. If you have a choice, however, here are some things to consider:

- *Lighting.* You should be able to see your screen clearly, without any glare. Bright sunlight can completely block out everything on the display, so it is a good idea to have shades on all windows. Also, you need good light for seeing the materials you keep on your desk, such as notes and documents. A desk light works better for this purpose than overhead lighting, which can contribute to glare.

- *Work space.* There should be plenty of room on the top of the desk or table where you place the PC. In addition to the computer, you need space for the keyboard, the mouse, a telephone, pens, pencils, notebooks, and other items you use during the day. Look into purchasing a desk made specifically for computers—they usually are designed to accommodate the different computer components, including drawers for the keyboard, and shelves for the printer and monitor. In addition, make sure the desk is sturdy. You do not want thousands of dollars worth of computer equipment crashing to the floor because a friend leans on your desk.

- *Accessibility.* The components should be set up where they can be reached easily, yet not where they are in the way of other activities. You do not want to fumble around to reach the disk drives, or worry about the dog bumping into the power switch.

- *Breathing room.* For the PC—not for you! There must be space for air to circulate around the PC, so that it does not overheat. Both the system unit and the monitor have fan vents that should not be blocked. Also, you need to leave space between the walls and the furniture for cables and wires.

Task lighting

Dedicated electrical outlets

Phone jacks for modem and network access

Adjustable seating

Ergonomic keyboard and mouse trays

- *Electricity*. At a minimum, you need to plug in the system unit and the monitor. Most other peripherals, including printers, modems, and external devices such as CD-ROM drives, also have their own plugs, which means that the more components you have, the more outlets you need. Rather than plug the components directly into a wall outlet, however, you should use a surge suppressor, or other device which can help protect your system from fluctuations in the electrical current. Because many PC failures are due to fluctuations in current, this component is very important. (You should not try to save money by neglecting to buy a surge suppressor.) These devices usually provide multiple outlets, as well.

- *Telephone lines*. If you have a modem, you should probably consider installing a separate phone line; that way, your telephone will be free, even when you are using your modem. If you do not have a modem, you still need a telephone outlet near your workspace, because you will probably want to keep a telephone handy. You can use a modem/phone line surge suppressor to help protect your modem from fluctuations in the phone line.

■ *Ergonomics.* That's a fancy word for comfort, and it's very important. You could end up spending a great deal of time in front of your PC, and you do not want to end up at the chiropractor's office. Get a comfortable chair that you can adjust. Ideally, you should be seated so that your lower arms are perpendicular to the floor when you type, and your eyes are level with the screen.

Attach a glare guard and adjust
monitor height to reduce eyestrain.

Maintain good
posture and
keep your feet
on the floor to
reduce strain on
neck, shoulders,
and back.

Use wrist rests and adjustable
keyboards to support your wrists at
the correct angle for typing.

Place your feet flat
on the floor.

Setting Up Your Computer

Before you buy your computer, technicians at the factory or the store where you purchase the equipment usually install all the necessary system software and internal hardware components, and maybe even some software applications. Then, they put the computer through a burn-in period to make sure that everything works.

The burn-in period consists of running a nonstop series of tests, called diagnostics. Once they determine that the computer works properly, they take the basic components apart so they can pack it up into boxes and deliver it to you.

When you get the computer, you need to unpack the boxes and connect the components so you can get them to work.

Unpacking

When you unpack the PC, open each
box carefully, and put the components
near the place where you intend to set
them up. You do not want to have to
move the system once you have hooked
it together. Keep the cables together
with the device they came with, and
look for installation or hook up
instructions that might help you
identify the ports and plugs you
need to use.

Position the devices on the
workspace so that you
can easily reach and
adjust all of the ports and cables. Most ports are on the back of the system
unit, but on some units, certain peripherals, such as a keyboard, often plug
into the front.

Did You Get What You Ordered?

Unless you are present when the dealer puts
your system in the carton, it is not
always easy to be sure you
receive the items you
ordered. The following
tips show you how to
make sure you got what
you paid for:

> **NOTE** ▼
>
> If possible, keep the original packing
> materials that the computer components
> come in. If you ever need to move the
> computer, you will have good, strong
> boxes that are the right size and well
> padded.

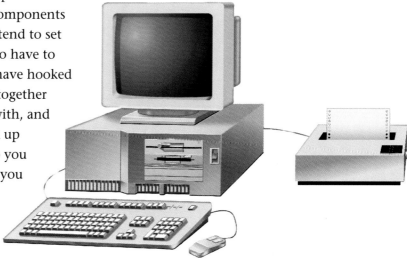

Monitor port and cable

Modem port and cable

System unit power cord

Keyboard port and cable

Printer port and cable

- Compare the information on the packing slip to the information on your order slip. On the packing slip, check off each component as you take it out of the box. Look for warranty cards and documentation for each component, and check the product numbers to be sure you have the right item. This is particularly important for internal components, such as video cards, which you cannot see.

- When you finally get around to starting the computer, watch the information that appears on-screen. In many cases, information about internal devices and software programs—such as version numbers and the amount of installed memory—is displayed. This is one way to verify that the dealer installed the correct internal components.

Connecting the Cables

Most peripherals can plug into only one particular port. To find the right one, look at the plug, and compare it with the ports. When you find the right port, attach the cable securely. In some cases, you may need to use a small screwdriver to tighten the screws on both sides of the port. (For more information about ports, plugs, and cables, see the section "What You Need to Know About Expansion" in Part III, "Understanding What Makes Your Computer Work.")

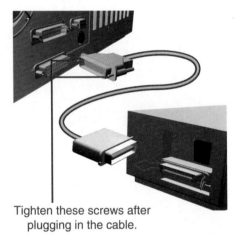

Tighten these screws after plugging in the cable.

Here are some other guidelines for connecting the cables:

- Only one cable comes from the system unit—the power cord.

- Two cables come from most monitors: one is a power cord and the other attaches to the video adapter port on the system unit.

- Two cables come from most printers: one is a power cord and the other attaches to the printer port on the system unit.

- One cable comes from the keyboard. It attaches to the keyboard port on the system unit.

■ One cable comes from the mouse. It attaches to a port on the system unit.

■ If you have a modem, plug one end of a phone wire into the jack marked "line" on the system unit (internal modems) or the modem itself (external modems), and the other end into the phone jack in the wall. To use a telephone on the same line as an internal modem, do the above, then plug one end of another phone wire into the jack marked "phone" on the system unit, and the other end into the telephone.

When all of the components are correctly attached to one another, plug all power cords into a surge suppressor. Then, plug the surge suppressor into an electrical wall outlet and turn on the surge suppressor by flipping the switch on top of it. You should see the light on the suppressor go on. Now, you are ready for action!

Starting Your Computer

Now that you have everything set up and ready to go, take a few minutes to look things over. Follow these steps:

> **NOTE** ▼
>
> Do not plug anything into an electrical outlet until you have connected all of the components.

1 Locate the power switches on the system unit, and on all peripherals. Most power switches are marked on one side with a straight line like this: |, which represents *On*, and on the other side with a circle, like this :/O, which represents *Off*. Some devices may have power buttons, which push in to turn on and push out to turn off.

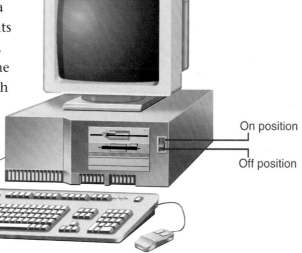

On position

Off position

2 Locate the brightness and contrast controls on the monitor, and adjust them somewhere in the middle. If they are turned all the way down (to the right) when you start your PC, you will think something is wrong with the computer, because your screen will be black.

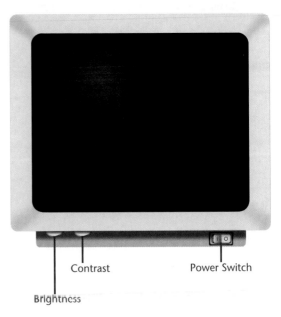

Contrast   Power Switch

Brightness

NOTE ▼

If a message appears telling you that there's a "non-system disk" in the disk drive. check drive A to make sure it's empty. If a message appears telling you that the PC can't find the operating system, contact your dealer immediately! See the upcoming section "Troubleshooting the Startup" for more information.

3 Turn on the surge suppressor or other power device to which your PC is attached.

4 Turn on the system unit by gently pressing the power switch until it clicks into the On position. Then, gently press the power switches on the monitor, the printer, and other external peripherals until they click into the On position.

What Happens During Startup

As soon as the power is on, the PC begins running a power-on self-test (POST) to make sure that all components are in working order.

NOTE ▼

If you have a lot of power switches to turn on and off, you might consider using the surge suppressor or other power protection device as a main switch. That way, you can leave all of the power switches in the On position all of the time. To turn off the PC, you turn off the power device. To turn on the PC, you turn on the power device.

You probably will hear the system come to life with some hums, clicks, and whirrs as the power supply's fan starts, and as the CPU counts the memory, checks components, and accesses the disk drives.

On the monitor, the CPU may display the name of some of the components it finds, and how much memory is available.

When the POST is complete, the CPU looks for the operating system. It always looks in drive A first, so the drive A in-use light goes on. If there is no disk in drive A, the CPU looks on hard drive C, so the hard disk in-use light goes on.

What you see next depends on how the PC is set up and what operating system you have.

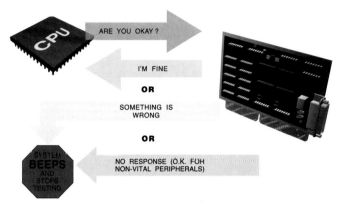

- If your PC has Windows 95, and Windows 95 successfully loads into memory, you see the Windows 95 desktop.

- If your PC has DOS, but does not have an automatic clock/calendar, a message appears on-screen asking you to confirm the current date and time, or to enter the correct date and time. Press the Enter key to continue.

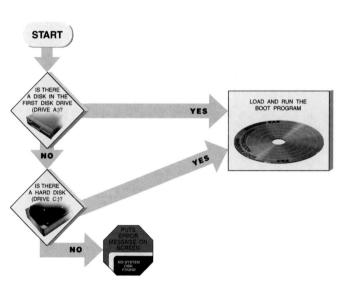

- If your PC has DOS and does have an automatic clock/calendar, your PC processes the commands in some DOS startup files. You may see messages on-screen telling you what is happening, or you may see nothing at all.

- If your PC has DOS, and DOS successfully loads into memory the DOS prompt appears on-screen.

- If someone has added a command to your AUTOEXEC.BAT to start an operating environment, such as Windows, or a customized menu system, that environment is displayed on-screen, instead of the DOS prompt.

Troubleshooting the Startup

If the CPU finds any problems during the POST, it may beep, or display an error message. If your computer stops, and displays an error message, write down the message. You can look for the message in the manual that came with the computer, or in Que's *Using DOS*, to see what it means, or you can call your dealer or a computer technician.

If the CPU completes the POST, but does not find an operating system, you may see this message:

```
Non-system disk or disk error
Replace and strike any key when ready.
```

If you see this message, check to be sure there is no disk in drive A (if the operating system is installed on drive C) or that the disk in drive A has the operating system on it (if the operating system is installed on a floppy disk). Then press any key to start the computer again.

NOTE ▼

If you see a message telling you that no operating system was found, contact the dealer, manufacturer, or a computer technician. You must install an operating system before you can use your PC.

Here are some other things to check if you have problems starting your computer:

1 Are all components connected firmly to the correct ports?

2 Are all components plugged into a power source?

3 Is the power source turned on?

4 Are all components turned on?

5 Are the brightness and contrast controls on the monitor adjusted correctly?

If necessary, shut everything off, wait a few minutes, and try turning the PC on again. Watch and listen to see if you can pinpoint the problem. Here are some of the things to watch for:

1 Listen for the hum of the fan in the system unit. If you do not hear it, the power supply may not be working.

2 Watch the monitor. If you do not see anything on-screen, the monitor may be broken, or the controls may need adjusting.

3 If the monitor is working, watch to see if the memory count is displayed. If not, the CPU is not completing the POST correctly.

4 If the disk in-use lights do not go on, the CPU is not completing the POST correctly, or the drives are damaged.

5 If the keyboard on-line status indicator does not light up, the CPU is not completing the POST correctly, the keyboard is damaged, or maybe the plug isn't attached firmly.

Troubleshooting Peripherals

If you have problems with a peripheral device, such as your modem, printer, CD-ROM drive, and so on, here are some of the things to check:

- Are all cables firmly and correctly attached?

- Is everything plugged in?

- Are all power switches turned on?

- Is the device's on-line or power light on?

- For a printer, check that the paper is loaded correctly.

- For a modem, check that the telephone lines are connected correctly.

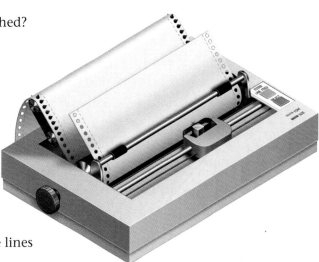

- If you hear an incessant beeping, wait, or shut the system off and try starting again. Something may have been pressing down on a key on the keyboard.

Caring for Your Computer

You should care for your PC the same way you care for any sensitive, high-priced appliance. Here is a list of some of the steps you can take to make sure that your computer lasts for a long time:

- Use a power protection device.

- Unplug components when they aren't in use.

- Keep food and drinks away from your computer.

- Maintain a consistent, moderate temperature in the room where the PC is located.

- Keep the PC clean. A cover helps keep dust from building up inside the system unit and the peripherals. You can vacuum the keyboard, and external parts of peripherals, and you can use a clean cloth and glass cleaner on the exterior surfaces of the system, such as the screen.

- Insure the PC.

- Keep records of the serial numbers of all components, including software.

- Send in all warranty and registration cards.

- Take care of your floppy disks. Do not leave them in the heat (they'll melt), and don't store them near electrical devices that have a magnetic field. Label them using a felt-tip pen so that you always know what they contain. Write-protect disks that contain information you do not want to erase, or overwrite (see "Handling Floppy Disks" in Part III to find out how to do this).

Moving Your Computer

If you have to move your computer, carefully follow these steps:

1 Make sure that every device is turned off. This includes external peripherals such as modems, printers, and CD-ROM drives.

2 Unplug every device.

3 Carefully disconnect the cables that connect the devices to the system unit. You can label the plugs and ports with masking tape so that you can easily reconnect them.

4 Put the cardboard drive protector that came with the PC—or an old, unnecessary disk—into the floppy drive(s) to protect the drive. Although it would take a significant jolt—like a dive from a second floor window— to damage the drive, it's better to be safe than sorry.

5 Most hard disks automatically *park* in a safe position when not in use (stop with the head positioned out of harm's way). However, if you have an old hard disk you may need to use a disk-parking utility to be sure that the drive head will not damage data on the disk during the move. To find out if your hard disk parks itself, refer to the setup section of the instructions that came with your computer, or contact your dealer.

6 If you are moving farther than the other side of the room, pack each device securely in its original box, or another well-padded box.

Understanding Power Protection

Like all electrical appliances, a PC can be damaged by changes to the power source. Both your hardware and software are vulnerable to power surges, fluctuations, and outages.

Here are a few things you can do to keep your system safe:

■ Always use a power protection device.

■ Unplug all components, including phone lines, during thunder and lightning storms. If lightning strikes the building or the power lines while the equipment is plugged in, the equipment can be ruined.

■ Save and back up your work. The only insurance against losing data due to power failures, is to store the information on disk, and to copy it onto floppy disks or backup cassette tapes frequently.

You should never plug a PC component directly into a wall outlet. Here are some of the devices you should consider using, instead:

Type	Benefits
Surge Suppressor	A surge suppressor (or spike suppressor) prevents damage from sudden changes in voltage, by filtering the current coming from the wall outlet. It does not protect the equipment from power outages. Phone/modem line suppressors do the same for telephone lines.
Uninterruptible power supply (UPS)	In addition to protecting a PC from power surges like a surge suppressor does, a UPS has its own battery which is activated in the event of a power failure. Before you lose data, you can save, and then shut off the equipment.
Power Bar	A power bar simply provides additional outlet connections. It offers no protection from power surges or power outages.

A surge suppressor   *An uninterruptible power supply*

Protecting Your Software and Data

Your software and data are perhaps the most vulnerable components of your PC. You can always buy a new hardware device but it is almost impossible to re-create lost data, and the loss of a software program can mean hours of downtime.

To safeguard your data against loss due to a power failure, you should establish a schedule for saving to disk while you are working. If you save every half-hour, any work you can lose will require, at most, half an hour to re-create. If you save every page, you know you will never lose more than a page's worth of work at a time. Some applications come with built-in saving utilities that automatically save, or prompt you to save, at certain intervals (which you can set according to what you prefer).

Even if you save religiously, there are other potential threats to data and to software. Disks and disk drives can be damaged, destroyed, or just worn out. There is only one way to safeguard your data against a disk failure: back up, back up, back up! There is no way to know how important a current set of backup disks is until you face a crisis. If you do not have backups you will spend hours—maybe even days—trying to re-create lost data.

To back up your data, you simply copy the data from your hard disk to floppy disks or tapes that can be removed from the drive and stored in a safe place. You can copy individual files, or entire portions of your hard disk. There are many different backup strategies; you can find one that suits your work style (see "Copying, Moving, and Deleting Files" in Part VI).

Windows 95 and DOS both come with built-in backup utilities, and other backup utilities are available. You should make backup copies of all the software program disks that you buy, and you should get into the habit of backing up the files you are working on at least once a day. For added security, keep backup copies of important data and programs in a safe place away from your PC, such as in a fireproof safe, or in a safety deposit box at your bank.

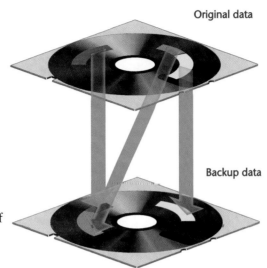

Original data

Backup data

A more insidious threat to your data is a software *virus*. Software viruses are programs that are written by troublemakers to wreak havoc on your computer system. The results of a virus may be as benign as displaying an unwanted message on your screen, or as malignant as destroying everything on your hard disk.

Some of the more common ways of catching a virus are from using an infected program or floppy disk, and from copying a program off of another computer on a network. You can protect your PC from viruses by following these practices:

- Buy software only from a reputable dealer.

- Don't buy software if you suspect that the package has been opened.

- Don't download programs from a bulletin board service.

- Don't use programs that you get on disk from another user.

- Use an anti-virus software utility program to remove viruses from disks and from memory, and to alert you if changes in your system indicate that a virus may be present. DOS 6.X comes with an anti-virus utility you can use with DOS or with Windows 3.11, and others are available.

PC DOs and DON'Ts

Here is a brief reminder of some of the most important PC DOs and DON'Ts:

DOs

- Put some thought into the type of PC you need before you buy one.

- Check the system requirements for a software program before you buy it. Make sure that your computer has the necessary memory, space, and components to run the program. (See "How Much Memory Do You Need" in Part III.)

- Save your work frequently.

- Create backups of your data and programs.

- Turn off your computer only after you have exited all applications.

- Write down all error messages displayed on your screen.

- Label your disks.

- Use a power protection device.

- Register your software and return all warranty cards.

- Use a user's manual or other book.

- Store your disks in a safe place.

- Keep your computer clean and dry.

- Change your online service or network password frequently to guard against unauthorized use.

DON'Ts

- Don't try to attach any peripherals to your computer when it is turned on.

- Don't open the system unit unless you are very familiar and knowledgeable about the components of the system unit.

- Don't take apart the power supply.

- Don't take a disk out of a drive when the drive in-use light is on.

- Don't turn off the computer if a software application is running.

- Don't force a disk into a disk drive.

- Don't leave disks in overheated rooms or cars or in direct sunlight.

- Don't spill anything on a disk or on the PC. If you spill something on a disk, throw the disk away.

- Don't eat or drink at your computer.

- Don't open the metal shutter of a floppy disk or touch the surface of the disk itself.

- Don't use the original program disks to install or run a software program. Make backup copies first, in case the originals are damaged during installation.

- Don't use borrowed disks or downloaded programs until you run a virus check on them.

- Don't move a computer when the computer is on.

- Don't leave your monitor on for long periods of time unless you are using it or have a screen-saver utility—an image can actually burn into your display and leave "ghosts" and shadows that never go away.

- Don't try to format your hard disk yourself.

- Don't put your printer on a table or cart that has wheels—the printer may vibrate when you use it and end up sliding around the room causing damage.

- Don't give out your credit card numbers or passwords to anyone on a computer network or online service.

PART III

Understanding What Makes Your Computer Work

What's Inside the System Unit

The *system unit* is the case, or box, that contains the electronic components that make your computer work. The system unit generally contains power supplies, one or more disk drives, and circuit cards or boards that control the system peripherals. Most importantly, the system unit houses the *motherboard*, the circuit card to which the central processing unit (CPU) is attached. The CPU is the microprocessor chip that controls the actual computing your PC performs.

If you take the top off a basic desktop PC system unit, you see some of the components shown in this illustration.

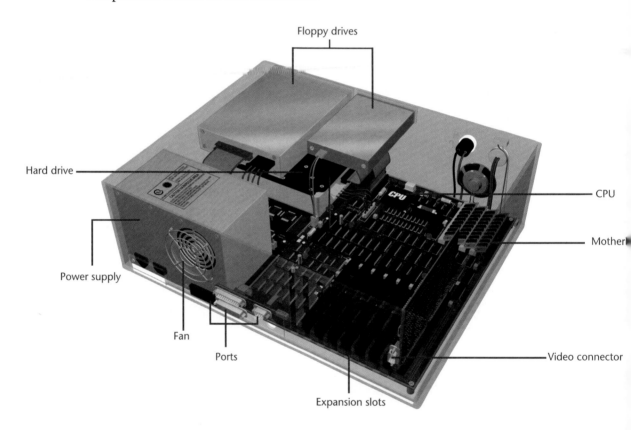

Floppy drives

Hard drive

CPU

Mother▪

Power supply

Fan

Ports

Video connector

Expansion slots

Although you should avoid opening your PC's system unit, the more you know about the components in it, the more prepared you will be to make a smart decision when you need to buy new equipment or get old equipment repaired.

The Motherboard

The *motherboard* is the main circuit board in the system unit. The most important electronic components, such as the *central processing unit*, or CPU (the chip that controls the PC's computing functions), and the *random access memory*, or RAM (the chips that make up a temporary storage area where the PC can keep information it is working with), are built into the motherboard. All other components, such as disk drives, are attached to the motherboard, so they can send information back and forth.

The motherboard has sockets, called *expansion slots* (or just slots), where you can plug in additional circuit boards, called *expansion cards*. The number of expansion slots depends on the size of your system unit. Most system units have a disk controller card and a video adapter card. You can purchase and plug in expansion cards for additional components, such as an internal modem card, an internal fax card, or a sound card.

If you need more RAM than is already installed in your PC, the motherboard usually also has slots where you can plug in memory expansion cards, called *SIMMs* (Single Inline Memory Modules). Most motherboards also have a slot for a *math coprocessor* chip: an electronic circuit that helps programs that use a lot of graphics or math equations run faster.

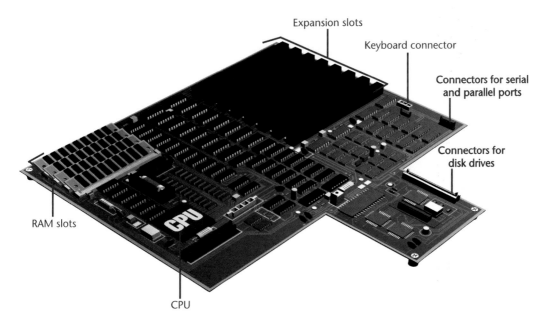

Expansion slots

Keyboard connector

Connectors for serial and parallel ports

Connectors for disk drives

RAM slots

CPU

The *CPU* is the computer's brain—a chip built into the motherboard that controls every computer instruction performed by the PC. It is the electronic circuit that performs the actual computing. Sometimes, the terms *CPU* and *microprocessor* are used interchangeably.

RAM stands for *random-access memory*. RAM is the electronic memory where the computer stores information while it is being used. RAM is not permanent; when the computer is turned off, all information stored in RAM is lost unless you first save it on a disk.

Chips are the tiny integrated circuits that control computer functions. The microprocessor is a chip. The math coprocessor is a chip. Memory is contained on chips. Some chips are built into circuit boards and others can be plugged into expansion slots on the circuit boards.

The Power Supply

The *power supply* converts the AC electricity from an outlet in your home or office to the DC electricity the PC uses. The computer's on/off switch is connected to the power supply.

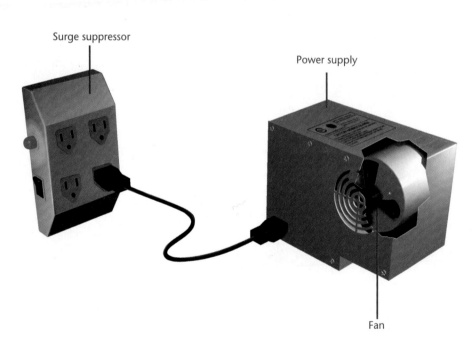

Surge suppressor

Power supply

Fan

Like light bulbs, the capacity of a power supply is measured in watts. 230 watts is just about right for the average PC, although some may need only 150 watts while others need up to 350 watts. If you ever have to replace your power supply, ask your dealer how many watts your particular power supply uses. A fan keeps the power supply and the other components in the system unit from overheating.

Because most PCs plug into a standard electrical outlet, they can be adversely affected by changes in the electrical current. It is a good idea to plug the PC into a *surge suppressor* or an *uninterruptible power supply* rather than plugging it directly into the wall outlet. Power protection is discussed in greater detail in the section "Caring for Your Computer" in Part II.

Microprocessors

Microprocessors are the electronic circuits (or chips) that control the computer by directing the flow of information to the appropriate component. The CPU is a microprocessor, and other microprocessors help move information to and from the CPU.

PCs are built around a family of microprocessors developed by Intel Corp. Every few years or so, a new generation of processors is developed that can process more information, and process it faster, than the previous generation. Traditionally, Intel identified its microprocessors with numbers, such as 80386 and 80486. (The computers these chips go into are referred to as "386" and "486," respectively.) Educated consumers know that the chips with the higher numbers are newer and more powerful. However, it's easier to trademark a name than a number, so Intel named its most recent microprocessor "Pentium" instead of 80586.

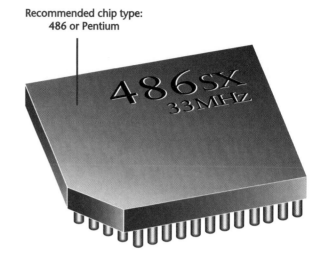

Recommended chip type:
486 or Pentium

NOTE ▼

To find out the minimum processor requirements for your applications, look on the back of the application package.

The newer, more powerful chips also cost more, but the additional processing power is usually worth the price. It is a good idea to buy a PC with the most powerful microprocessor you can afford. Chip technology evolves quickly, so even the second most powerful microprocessor may soon be obsolete.

Newer chips usually are *downwardly compatible* with the older chips, which means that software programs written to run on computers with the older chips can be run on computers with the newer chips. The older chips, however, may not be able to run programs written for the newer chips.

Here are some questions to keep in mind when selecting a microprocessor:

■ What kinds of software will you run? Some software programs, such as Windows or Microsoft Word, run better on—and may even require—a faster processor.

■ Will you do a lot of number crunching? Programs that perform mathematical calculations (such as CAD and database programs) require a math coprocessor to run efficiently. Math coprocessors are chips installed on the motherboard and are designed specifically to relieve the CPU of the burden of performing mundane calculations.

■ How much can you afford? Even if you don't think you need the most powerful chip available today, you should buy the most advanced computer that you can afford. Developments in technology quickly make older, slower chips obsolete.

> **NOTE** ▼
>
> Many PCs are built with chips that can be upgraded in the future. If you think your processing needs are going to increase, or you just want to be ready to take advantage of improvements in technology, you should consider buying a PC that can be upgraded.

Decoding the Chip Number

Processor type	Usage
8088	The first PCs ran on these CPUs.
80286	Still running a large number of installed PCs, IBM based its AT-class PCs on the 80286.
80386	PCs with an 80386 CPU are able to run most software programs, but may become somewhat outdated with the introduction of the Windows 95 operating system.
80486	PCs manufactured today have at least an 80486 CPU.
80586, or Pentium	PCs based on the Pentium are fast becoming the standard. This newest generation of microprocessors more than doubles the performance of the fastest 80486 microprocessors.

What Are SX, DX, and So On?

Microprocessors are also differentiated by type or version. Each version is better suited for specific uses, depending on how it processes information, and on what built-in features it has. The letters that designate the chip type help describe the applications for which the chip should be used.

SX chips usually run more slowly than DX chips. 386SX chips use a 16-wire bus instead of a 32-wire bus, which means instructions are carried over 16 wires instead of over 32 wires. 486SX and Pentium SX chips do not have a functioning math coprocessor. SX chips usually are less expensive than DX chips, so they are better suited to casual or home use.

DX chips usually process information faster than SX chips. 386DX chips use a 32-wire bus, which is more efficient than a 16-wire bus. 486DX and Pentium DX chips have a built-in math coprocessor for enhancing the perform-ance of scientific or mathematical calculations. DX chips are suitable for most business uses.

Other chip designations include DX2 and SL. DX2 chips operate at twice the speed of DX chips. For example, a DX2/66 runs at 66 MHz internally (when performing calculations), but communicates externally (with the rest of the computer hardware) at half that, or 33 MHz. But don't fret. The ability to communicate at twice the "normal" speed gives the DX2 almost double the average performance of a non-DX2 chip. DX2 chips are usually used for heavy-duty information processing. SL chips, which are designed to conserve energy, usually are used in portable PCs.

> **NOTE** ▼
>
> The processor speed is usually included in the name of the processor. For example, if you see an ad for a 486DX 66, it means the 486DX runs at 66MHz.

> **Why Speed Is Important**
>
> How fast a computer processes information depends on the type of microprocessor, the chip's clock speed, and the amount of available memory. Sometimes, the difference in speed is barely noticeable, but most software programs run better on a PC with a faster processor and a faster clock speed. If you try to run Windows 95 on a PC with a 386 processor at any clock speed, you will spend a lot of time waiting for a task to be accomplished. When you run Windows 95 on a PC with a 486DX 66 or a Pentium, however, programs move at a quick and smooth pace.

What about Speed?

Computer *speed* refers to how fast the CPU can process information—or turn input into output. Each microprocessor contains a *clock*. The clock that controls the microprocessor speed is not the same as the clock that keeps track of the current date and time, however. The faster the clock "ticks," the faster the computer functions are processed. Microprocessor speeds are measured in *megahertz* (MHz).

CPUs can run at different speeds. An 80486 microprocessor, for example, may run at 25MHz, 33MHz, or 66MHz. Some Pentium processors run at 120MHz! Because newer chips are designed to outperform earlier models, they can run at slower clock speeds than older chips, and still process information at a faster rate. A Pentium running at 66MHz, for example, processes information faster than an 80486 running at 100MHz.

What Is Computer Memory?

Recommended RAM: 8 megabytes

Minimum RAM: 4 megabytes

Memory is the electronic circuitry where the PC stores information while it is in use, including programs and data. There are two types of memory used by all PCs: *RAM* and *ROM*. Both are stored on chips attached to the motherboard.

RAM stands for *random-access memory*, which is memory that is constantly being used and reused by the computer. RAM is kind of like a blackboard in a classroom—information is written on it, erased, and written on it again.

ROM stands for *read-only memory*, which is memory that you cannot erase or write on. ROM provides the instructions a computer needs to get started each time you turn it on.

SIMMS attach to the motherboard

PCs come with different amounts of RAM, and you can add more RAM if needed. The amount of ROM a computer has is determined by its manufacturer. You cannot increase ROM. For practical purposes, the only kind of memory you need to be concerned with is RAM.

Why RAM Is Important

RAM is contained on memory chips installed on the motherboard. On older PCs, such as those based on the 8088 processor, each RAM chip is placed into a separate socket. On newer PCs, RAM chips are sold attached to a standard memory add-in card called a *Single In-line Memory Module*, or SIMM. SIMMs generally hold eight or nine RAM chips, but some hold three.

To a certain degree, the amount of RAM you have installed determines which application programs you can run. You must have enough RAM to store the application *and* process data. The more complex the application is, the more RAM it uses.

Measuring Memory

Memory is measured in bytes. (So is storage space, which you can learn about in the section "Understanding Data Storage," coming up later in this part.) Each *byte* is roughly the equivalent of one keyboard character. A *kilobyte* (abbreviated K) equals a little more than a thousand characters. A *megabyte* (M) equals a little more than a million characters. A *gigabyte* (G) equals a little more than a billion characters. Once, 512K of memory was considered a lot. Now, you need at least 4M of memory to run most applications! You can increase the amount of memory in your PC by plugging more memory chips or SIMM boards into the motherboard.

How PCs Use Memory

Just adding memory to your PC may not be enough to boost performance. The way a PC uses memory also depends on the type of microprocessor in the PC, the operating system, and the software program (or programs) the PC is running.

Save Your Work!

RAM is short-term memory, which means it isn't designed for permanent data storage. Data stored in the computer's memory is always at risk, because if you lose power, you lose everything currently in memory. To permanently save information, you need to copy the information onto a hardware storage device, such as a floppy disk or your hard drive. That's why disk drives are important. When you save your data to disk, it is copied from memory. Even if the data is lost from RAM, you can recall it from the disk.

As you work with your PC, you should always remember that RAM is not permanent! All data stored in RAM is lost when:

- You shut off your PC.
- You reset your PC.
- You close the current application program.
- You lose power.

NOTE ▼

Measurements in bytes are rounded off to numbers that computers—and people!—can work with easily. Really, 1K of memory is equal to 1,024 bytes. When someone says his computer has 1M of memory, for example, it actually has 1,048,576 bytes

All PCs running DOS use only the first 640K of memory for running the operating system and application programs, and for storing data—no matter how much memory is installed, or how fast a processor they are using.

Many programs are too large to fit into 640K at one time. Waiting for the instructions to be swapped back and forth from a disk is not practical, so computer technicians figured out how to make some PCs use memory beyond the first 640K for temporarily storing information.

As a result, the amount of RAM available for use on a PC is now classified into three basic categories:

- Conventional memory

- Upper memory

- Extended, or high, memory

NOTE ▼

In theory, computers using Windows 95 (or another 32-bit operating system like OS/2 or Windows NT) are not limited by the 640K conventional memory barrier. However, the way the application software programs running under these operating systems are written also effects their ability to access all available memory.

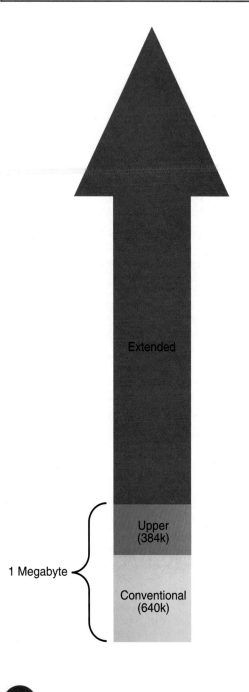

Extended

Upper
(384k)

1 Megabyte

Conventional
(640k)

Conventional memory is the first 640K of RAM, which all DOS-based PCs use for processing information. The amount of conventional memory that is available for processing affects the speed at which programs will run. If, for example, the operating system is using a percentage of available conventional memory, application programs will run more slowly because more of the instructions must be stored on disk. Today, most PCs have the maximum 640K of conventional memory installed, but they can have less.

Upper memory is all the memory between conventional memory (the first 640K) and 1024K (1M). PCs based on an 80286 or higher microprocessor can use upper memory for temporarily storing information. The operating system and some memory-resident utilities, for instance, can be moved into upper memory, freeing conventional memory for running applications. All information is still processed in the first 640K, but swapping information from upper memory to conventional memory is faster than swapping it from a disk to conventional memory.

Extended (or *high*) *memory* is all memory over 1M. It is called extended memory because it provides storage capacity beyond the original limitation of 1M. Theoretically, some PCs can address up to 4G of memory, but buying that much would cost over $100 million. 16M and 32M are more common configurations.

How Much Memory Do You Need?

Different software programs require different amounts of memory in order to run correctly. Check the software package or the documentation to find out how much memory a program needs before you buy it, and whether a program can use extended memory. Microsoft, for example, says that to run Windows 3.1 you should have at least 2M of memory. To run Windows 95, you need at least 4M, but 8M is preferable.

Even if you don't need it now, it's a good idea to buy a computer that can be expanded to hold at least 32M of RAM.

Figuring Out How Much Memory You Have

To find out how much memory your computer has, do one of the following:

- Watch the monitor when you start up. As the PC checks the memory, it displays the number of bytes installed.

- If you use DOS, use the MEM command. It displays a chart of all types of memory installed, how much is being used, and how much is available (see "Checking Your System Memory" in Part VII).

- If you use Windows 95, look in the System Properties dialog box (right-click the My Computer icon and choose Properties from the shortcut menu. Then click on the Performance tab). It lists the amount of memory and the percentage of available memory.

NOTE ▼

On a software package, you usually see both the minimum memory requirements for running the program and the recommended memory requirements. The minimum memory requirements are just that—the least amount of memory needed to run the program. The recommended memory requirements tell you the whole story—how much memory the program needs to run smoothly and efficiently. Follow the recommended requirements whenever possible.

Type **mem** at the C:\ prompt

DOS lists your system memory here

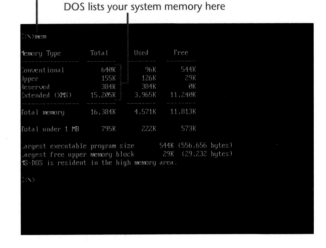

Installed memory   Percentage of free resources

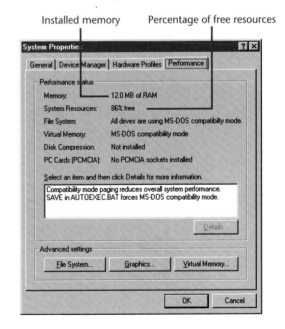

More Kinds of Memory

The performance of some PC hardware and software can be improved by making other kinds of memory available. For example, you aren't limited to using Conventional memory just because you have an older system model. Here are a few kinds of memory that can be used to boost performance on many PCs:

- Expanded memory is a combination of hardware and software that lets PCs based on the 8088 microprocessor access memory over the 640K conventional memory limit, and up to 32M. The system tricks the PC into thinking that this additional memory is really conventional memory. (Because this system was set up by Lotus, Intel, and Microsoft, you may hear software that uses expanded memory called LIM-compatible.)

  Some software programs, such as the release 2.X versions of Lotus 1-2-3, use expanded memory instead of extended memory. Systems based on the 80386, 80486, and Pentium processors can convert a certain amount of extended memory to expanded memory for applications that require this older form of high memory.

- Cache memory is made up of additional memory chips that are built right into the CPU or added externally to the CPU. Cache memory can boost the PC's processing speed because commonly used instructions that are stored on disk drives or in RAM are made available to the CPU at all times. You don't have to wait while the CPU swaps information in and out of RAM. How much cache memory improves your PC's performance depends mostly on the type of applications you are running. All programs will benefit somewhat, but large, complex programs will benefit the most. 80486 and Pentium processors generally come with at least 8K of built-in cache memory. If you plan to run large spreadsheets or relational database programs, you may want to consider 256K of cache!

- Video memory is made up of additional memory chips built right into the video display adapter card that controls your monitor. The amount of video memory determines how many colors can be displayed and how quickly images will appear. If you plan to run applications that display graphics, you should purchase a video adapter card that comes with built-in memory or that has room for memory to be added.

Understanding Data Storage

If computers could keep data only in RAM, they would not be of much use. When you shut off the PC or changed applications, all the data would be erased. You would quickly decide that returning to pencil and paper was easier—and safer!

Storage devices enable you to store programs and data for future use. When you enter the correct command, the PC writes the data it has in memory onto the storage device. The data stays there, available to be read or changed, until you enter a command to overwrite it or erase it.

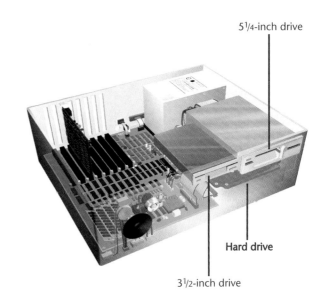

5¹/₄-inch drive

Hard drive

3¹/₂-inch drive

The most common type of storage device is a magnetic disk, either hard or floppy. Magnetic tape cartridges and optical disks are also used with PCs.

Most PCs come with at least one hard disk drive and one floppy disk drive. Nowadays, you usually get a CD-ROM drive as well. A standard configuration, for example, includes one 3¹/₂-inch floppy drive, one hard disk drive, and one CD-ROM drive. PCs can contain more than one disk drive and more than one type of disk drive. Your PC, for example, might have one hard drive, one 5¹/₄-inch floppy drive, and one 3¹/₂-inch floppy drive. Your coworker's PC might have one hard drive and two 5¹/₄-inch floppy drives. Many PCs also have CD-ROM drives. There are many possibilities.

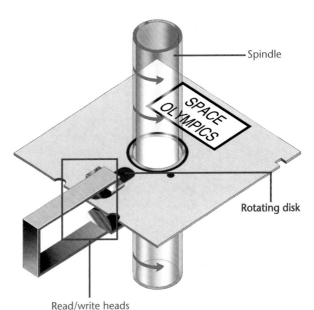

Spindle

SPACE OLYMPICS

Rotating disk

Read/write heads

How Disk Drives Work

Hard disk drives and floppy disk drives work in a similar manner. Each disk is coated with a magnetic material. Inside the drive, heads move across the rotating disk, reading and writing magnetic data. The heads move inward and outward along the spinning disk, picking up different tracks of information.

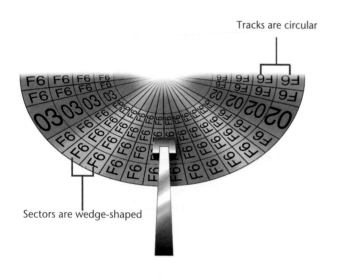

Tracks are circular

Sectors are wedge-shaped

Before a drive can read or write information on a disk, the disk must be formatted. Formatting electronically divides the disk into circular *tracks* and wedge-shaped *sectors*.

When you save data, the drive copies it onto the disk into a particular track and sector, then records the location in a *file allocation table*—or FAT—on the disk. When you enter a command to recall specific data, the drive consults the FAT to find the exact location; then it references the correct track and sector.

Think of formatting a disk as kind of like painting sections of a parking garage in different colors. You find your car by remembering the color of the floor level and the name of the section within the floor, maybe Blue E. On a disk, the drive finds your file by remembering the track and sector.

Hard disks should be formatted before you buy your PC. Floppy disks can be purchased formatted, or you can buy unformatted disks (which are slightly cheaper) and format them before you use them.

A Word about Drive Controllers

Communication between drives and the PC is handled by a disk drive controller chip. Some PCs have controllers built into the motherboard. Some controllers are on an expansion card that is attached to the motherboard. There are several standards that have developed for drive-to-controller communications, the most common of which are the Integrated Drive Electronics (IDE) standard and the Small Computer Systems Interface (SCSI—pronounced Skuzzy) standard.

Most PC hard disks communicate with the PC using the IDE standard. IDE drives attach to an interface card built directly into most motherboards, eliminating the need for an expansion card or special software. Each IDE interface can support up to eight drives, which is more than enough for most home and business applications.

The SCSI standard, however, is gaining popularity. SCSI and SCSI-2 controllers can be used to operate up to seven peripherals, including tape backup units and CD-ROM drives. SCSI-3 controllers can handle up to 16 devices! SCSI devices are, generally, significantly more expensive than IDE devices, but they offer more power. In order to use a SCSI drive, the PC must be equipped with a SCSI controller. Installing a SCSI controller requires an expansion card and special software.

NOTE ▼

Disk drives installed on your PC are identified using a naming scheme that relies on the letters of the alphabet. The first floppy drive is drive A. If you have a second floppy drive, it is drive B. The first hard drive is always called drive C, and so on. Each additional drive is referred to by the next letter in the alphabet. Usually, that means a CD-ROM drive is either D or E.

How Much Can a Disk Store?

The amount of data you can store on a disk is called *storage capacity*. Capacity, like memory, is measured in bytes. Hard disks hold from 20M to more than 9G! Floppy disks hold from 360K to 2.88M.

Remember that 1 byte equals about 1 character. So, assuming that you can fit 1,000 typed characters on a page, each 1K of storage space can hold about 1 page of information. Therefore, a 500M hard drive can hold about 500,000 pages!

What You Need to Know about Hard Disks

Hard disks can hold significantly more information than floppy disks, and they can spin much faster than floppy disks. Hard disks also are less easily damaged than floppies because they are fixed inside the drive, and therefore are less susceptible to damage by heat, dirt, and other external conditions.

WHY WORRY?

To safeguard information, you should always keep copies—called backups—of the information that you store on disks. Disks are mechanical and can fail or become damaged, or the people using them can make mistakes and delete or destroy information accidentally. You can store backup copies on other disks, or on tapes. For more information about protecting your data, see the section "Caring for Your Computer" in Part II.

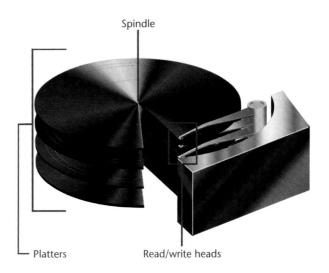

Spindle

Platters

Read/write heads

Most people use hard disks to store all of their programs and data, using floppy disks only to install new programs, make backup copies, or transfer data from one system to another.

Each hard disk drive contains many disks, or *platters*, all of which are used to store data. The platters spin on a single spindle while the read/write heads float between them. The heads never actually touch the platters, which is one reason hard disks can spin faster than floppies. Here are some things to keep in mind when you use a hard drive:

■ Avoid bumping or moving your computer when the disk drive in-use light is on (one of the LEDs on the front of the system unit). Hard disks can be damaged if the read and write heads in the drive touch the disk.

■ Secure your computer to prevent unauthorized use of the information stored on your hard disk. Use the lock that comes with the PC (however, sometimes the key to one computer will unlock another computer of the same brand, so this isn't foolproof), lock your office door, or invest in a security program that requires you to enter a password in order to access your data.

■ Back up the data from your hard disk to floppy disks or to tape. If something happens to your hard disk, at least your data will be safe.

■ Don't try to format a hard disk yourself. Take it to a professional computer technician.

What Size Hard Disk Should I Buy?

Hard disks are differentiated primarily by capacity. Most new systems come with a minimum hard drive capacity of 100M, but many are much larger than that.

The amount of storage space is the most important factor to consider when you are buying a hard disk drive. A good rule of thumb is to buy a hard drive that can hold at least twice as much as you think you need. Chances are your storage require-ments are going to increase, not decrease! Consider this: To install Windows 95 you need about 40M bytes of free disk space. To install the entire Microsoft Office for Windows 95 suite of programs, you need an additional 90M bytes! (Luckily, you don't have to install the whole Office suite—you can pick and choose the features you need, and it will take up less disk space if you do.)

How Fast Does My Hard Disk Need To Be?

The speed with which a disk drive can find information stored on its disk is called *average access time*. Average access time is measured in milliseconds (ms). One millisecond equals 1/1000 of a second. Most hard drives have average access times between 8ms and 20ms.

The speed with which a disk drive can transfer information from the disk into your computer's RAM is called the *transfer rate*. Transfer rates are measured in kilobytes per second (kps) or megabits per second. Typical transfer rates range from 2 to 5 megabits per second for IDE devices, and 5 to 10 megabits per second for SCSI devices.

You can speed up a hard drive's average access time by using a disk cache program. A disk cache program is software that tells the PC to keep a portion of RAM available so that data from the hard disk can be stored until the CPU needs it. That way, the CPU doesn't have to wait for the drive to find the data from the hard disk. MS-DOS and Windows (3.1 and 95) both come with built-in disk cache programs.

What You Need to Know about Floppy Disks

Floppy disks, also called diskettes or floppies, come in two sizes: 5¼-inch and 3½-inch. Disk drives are designed for one size or the other—you cannot put a 5¼-inch disk into a 3½-inch disk drive, or vice versa.

5¼-inch floppy disk

Write-protect notch

3½-inch floppy disk

Write-protect notch

To muddy the waters a bit, each size of disk comes in one of two densities: double density and high density. The density determines how much data can fit on a disk. High-density disks have higher capacities than double-density disks. Use this table to help figure out the density and capacity of each size of disk:

Disk Type	Capacity
5¼-inch	
Double-density (DD)	360K
High-density (HD)	1.2M
3½-inch	
Double-density (DD)	720K
High-density (HD)	1.44M
2.88 disks	2.88M

What Disks Should You Buy?

Basically, you should buy the disks that fit in the disk drives on your PC. Although you can easily tell the size of a disk just by looking at it, other disk qualities can be hard to spot. The safest way to be sure you buy the right kind is to read the box. You should always check the following information:

- Size

- Density

- Number of sides

- Formatted or unformatted

NOTE ▼

High-density drives can format, read, and write double-density disks, but double-density drives cannot format, read, or write high-density disks. You can tell what the density of a disk is by checking the label.

Sometimes manufacturers use abbreviations on the diskette box to identify the disk characteristics. Use the following table to decode the box:

On the Box	What It Means
DD	Double-density.
HD	High-density.
2 or DS	Double-sided.
1 or SS	Single-sided.
Preformatted IBM	The disks have been formatted for use with IBM-compatible PCs.
Preformatted Apple	The disks have been formatted for use with personal computers manufactured by Apple (such as the Macintosh).
Mini-floppy	For use in $5^1/_4$-inch drives.
Micro-floppy	For use in $3^1/_2$-inch drives.

NOTE ▼

If you choose to buy formatted diskettes, make sure they are formatted for the type of computer you own! Diskettes formatted for use on Apple or Macintosh computers must be reformatted for use on a PC!

Handling Floppy Disks

Be careful how you handle floppy disks! They can be damaged easily by dirt, heat, moisture, and unnecessary roughness. Here are some tips on how to handle floppy disks:

- The $5^1/_4$-inch disk can be bent or torn if you are not careful. Do not touch the areas such as the disk hub, where the disk is not covered by the protective jacket!

■ Keep disks away from heat and dirt, and do not store them too close to magnetic sources (including the PC if it has a hard drive in it, and paper clips that become magnetized by a magnetic paper clip holder).

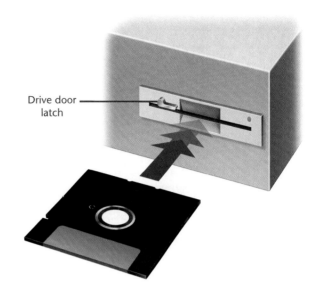

Drive door latch

■ Attach your own label to each disk so that you always know what is stored on it. Use a felt-tip pen to record information such as the date, the file, and program names, and whether the disk is formatted or not. (Using a ball-point pen can make indentations on the disk, rendering it unusable.)

■ When you insert a 5¼-inch disk into the disk drive, make sure it doesn't bend. Hold the disk with the label toward you, facing up. Slide it all the way in, then close the drive door latch. To remove the disk, open the drive door and slide the disk out.

■ Insert 3½-inch disks into the disk drive, metal shutter first, with the label facing up. 3½-inch drives do not have drive doors. Slide the disk in all the way until you hear a click and the disk removal button pops out. To remove the disk, press the disk removal button so that the disk slides easily out of the drive.

Disk removal button

■ Never force a disk into a disk drive! A disk should slide easily into the drive. Make sure that you are holding the disk the right way, and that another disk isn't already in the drive.

■ Never try to insert or remove a disk if the drive's in-use light is on.

■ You can protect important data stored on floppy disks by using write-protection. Both 5¼- and 3½-inch floppies can be write-protected, which means that the drive can read data from the disk but will not write any data onto the disk. To write-protect a 5¼-inch disk, cover the notch that appears on the upper-right corner of the disk with a piece of secure tape. To write-protect a 3½-inch disk, slide the write-protect tab (it's on the upper-left corner of the back of the disk) up to open the little window.

Write-protect notch on a
5¼-inch disk

Write-protect tab on a 3½-inch disk

> **NOTE** ▼
>
> If you try to write or save data onto a disk that has been write-protected, this message appears on-screen (the letter will be different depending on which drive you are using):
>
>   Write protect error writing drive A
>   Abort, Retry, Fail?
>
> Remove the disk and make sure that it is the one you want. If it is, then remove any write-protection, reinsert the disk, and type R. If this doesn't work, type F and try saving the data to a different disk.

What about Tape Drives?

You can use tape drives to read and write information to magnetic tape cartridges. Tapes are very useful for making backup copies of the data stored on a hard drive because the entire contents of a hard disk can fit on one tape, and because you can remove the tapes and put them in a safe place. If something happens to your disks, you still have all your data.

Tape cartridges are similar to the audio tape cartridges you might listen to in your car, and the tape drives work much like an audio tape player. Some tape drives can be attached to the PC inside the system unit, to a floppy disk drive controller card, or to an expansion card. Other tape drives are connected externally by cables to a port on the system unit.

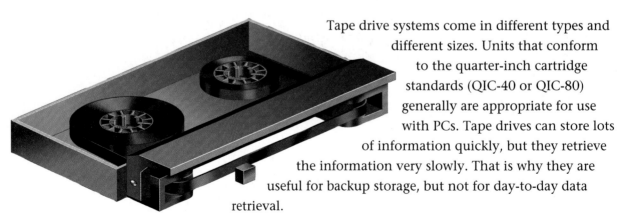

Tape drive systems come in different types and different sizes. Units that conform to the quarter-inch cartridge standards (QIC-40 or QIC-80) generally are appropriate for use with PCs. Tape drives can store lots of information quickly, but they retrieve the information very slowly. That is why they are useful for backup storage, but not for day-to-day data retrieval.

Like disks, tapes must be formatted before they can hold data. You can buy tapes preformatted.

What You Need to Know about CD-ROM Drives

CD-ROM stands for *Compact Disk, Read-Only Memory*. CD-ROM drives let you access large amounts of data stored on 5¼-inch platters, called *CD-ROMs*. One CD-ROM can hold up to 650M of data, which is much more than a typical hard disk can hold.

CD-ROM drives can be installed internally or attached externally to a port on the system unit. Originally, CD-ROM drives came in only one speed—*very slow*. Now double-speed, triple-speed, quad-speed, and even six-speed drives are available—with quad-speed drives the norm. Under no circumstances should you settle for less than a double-speed drive, and if you can afford a quad-speed drive, get it. Typically, quad-speed drives have a transfer rate of 600 kilobytes per second (kps), which is quadruple the speed of a single-speed drive.

PCs can access the data on CD-ROMs, but cannot write anything on them, which means that you cannot use a CD-ROM for backing up or storing your own files.

What You Can Do with a CD-ROM Drive

CD-ROM drives are becoming more and more popular because they can hold vast amounts of data in a variety of formats, and because they are reliable.

CD-ROMs are just like audio CDs, and many CD-ROM drives can be used to play the same CDs you play in your compact disc player at home or in the car (but not vice versa!). On computers, CD-ROMs are primarily used for installing new software applications, and for running and creating *multimedia applications*. CD-ROMs are suitable for multimedia applications because they can store and play back information in forms other than simple text. A CD-ROM, for example, can hold and play back audio (such as music), animation, and computer-generated graphics. You can learn more about multimedia applications in the section "What Is a Multimedia Computer" in Part IV.

CD-ROMs are also used to store large amounts of text, such as that of encyclopedias, telephone books, magazines, and periodicals. Often, these reference materials are enhanced by the inclusion of photos, animation, and sound.

Why You Might Benefit from a CD-ROM Drive

Some reasons why you might want to purchase a CD-ROM drive with your PC include:

■ The ability to run multimedia applications.

■ The ability to access large amounts of information from one source.

■ The future potential for more applications—CD-ROM technology is expanding at a rapid pace.

What to Look for in a CD-ROM Drive

If you already have a PC and are thinking of adding a CD-ROM drive, keep these things in mind:

■ You'll need at least a 386 microprocessor, 4M of RAM, and a 200M hard drive. The CD-ROM applications will run better on a 486 with 8M of RAM.

■ Although technically DOS can play CD-ROM applications, to get the most out of the CD-ROM applications, you should have at least Windows 3.1. However, Windows 95 is recommended because it has built-in multimedia support.

■ You need a sound card and speakers in your PC in order to hear the audio. An 8-bit sound card is adequate; a 16-bit sound card is preferred. You'll learn more about sound cards in the section "Sound Cards" in Part VI.

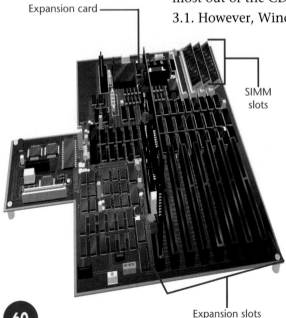

Expansion card

SIMM slots

Expansion slots

What You Need to Know about Expansion

Expandability is the amount of room available in a computer for adding extra hardware devices—peripherals or memory.

The expandability of a system unit depends on three things:

- The number and type of internal expansion slots.

- The number and type of external expansion ports.

- The number of available memory slots.

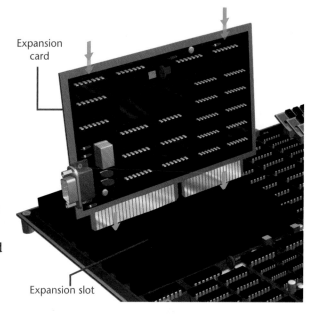

Expansion card

Expansion slot

Most people want to buy computers that have a lot of expandability because you will almost certainly need more computing power in the future than you need now. Because predicting how much computing power you will need—or even what kind of computing power will be available—is difficult, you can hedge your bets by purchasing a computer that has room for expansion.

For example, if you buy a PC with several open expansion slots, you can attach internal modems, fax boards, sound boards, and network controllers as needed. Also, as new technologies become available, you may be able to add them to your computer rather than purchase a new computer.

Expansion Slots and Expansion Cards

Expansion slots are sockets on the motherboard where you can attach expansion cards. *Expansion cards* are circuit boards containing the electronics that control peripherals or add memory. The words *board* and *card* are used interchangeably.

Mouse port

Some slots hold cards that control the basic system components, such as the video adapter card for the monitor and the disk controller card for the disk drives. You can't put another card, such as a modem, in one of the slots reserved for the basic system components.

Keyboard port

Depending on the size of your system unit, however, there may be slots left open even after the basic controller cards are installed. These open slots are the key to your computer's expandability.

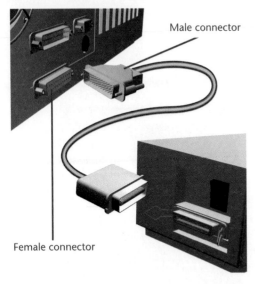

Male connector

Female connector

Ports

Ports are sockets on the outside of the system unit that are connected to the motherboard or to expansion cards on the inside of the system unit. You use cables to plug peripheral devices into ports. This way, peripherals and the PC can communicate.

Most PCs come with at least four ports for connecting devices such as a printer, a mouse, and the display monitor. Some PCs come with extra ports.

You cannot attach peripherals to just any port that happens to be available. For example, your monitor attaches to the video adapter port. You cannot plug a printer into the video adapter port; it won't fit and the printer won't work. The port on the system unit and the plug on the peripheral's cable must be compatible, which means both the size and type must match.

One way to tell with which port the plug works is by counting the number of connectors, or pins, it has. Look on the system unit for a port that corresponds in size to the plug on the cable. Also, look to see if the pins stick out (male connector) or in (female connector). If the pins on the plug stick out, the port must have corresponding sockets, and vice versa.

Connections are always between male and female connectors. You cannot plug a male cable into a male port, or a female cable into a female port.

The following list describes the types of ports available on PCs:

■ Parallel ports send all data synchronously, one byte at a time through eight separate wires in a cable. Parallel ports usually are designated LPT (an abbreviation for line printer). If the computer has one parallel port, it is called LPT1; a second parallel port is called LPT2, and so on. Parallel ports are used primarily for attaching printers because they cannot transmit data efficiently over long distances. Most parallel ports use DB-25 connectors, which have 25-pins. They are used commonly for external tape backup units and CD-ROMs, as well as for printers.

25-pin parallel connector

- Serial ports send data through one wire. These ports transfer data more slowly than parallel ports, but more effectively over long distances. Some serial ports have 9-pin connectors; some have 25-pin connectors. Serial ports are sometimes called *RS-232* ports and usually are designated *COM* (short for communications). If your computer has one serial port, it is called COM1; a second serial port is called COM2, and so on. Serial ports are commonly used for attaching serial printers (printers that use a serial connection), modems, and mice.

- A video adapter port is used for attaching a monitor to the video adapter card inside the system unit. Video adapter ports are designed for a specific type of video display adapter card. Some ports have 9-pin connectors and some have 15-pin connectors. For example, a VGA adapter always uses a 15-pin, three-row connector, while EGA and CGA—older adapters—use a 9-pin, two-row connector. The plug from a monitor must be compatible with the type of video adapter card you have.

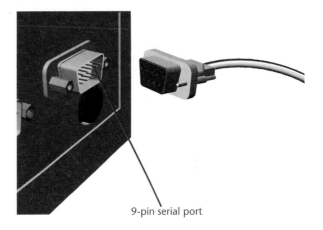

9-pin serial port

- A SCSI port lets you transfer data at high speeds. SCSI ports are used to attach SCSI-compatible devices, such as external hard disks, tape backup units, or CD-ROM drives. You can attach up to eight SCSI devices to one SCSI port (although the controller often counts as one device, thus leaving seven available). SCSI ports are not as common as the other port types, partly because SCSI devices usually are expensive.

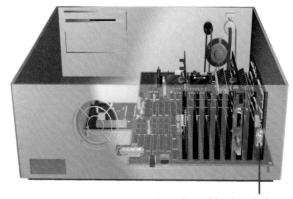

The video cable plugs in here

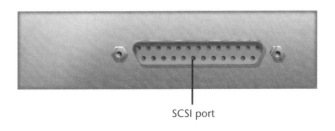

SCSI port

■ A game port is used for attaching a joystick device to the system unit. A game port has 15 pins. Joysticks are attached to game ports because they are commonly used for playing games.

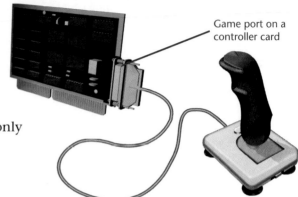

Game port on a controller card

What Is a Bus?

Expansion slots on the motherboard are sometimes called the expansion bus or the system bus. A *bus* is a set of wires or conductors that the expansion cards and the peripherals use to communicate with the processor.

There are different types of buses, so there are different types of expansion bus slots. When you buy an expansion card, make sure the card is compatible with the type of expansion bus in your computer. To find out what kind of bus you have, check the original packing slip that came with your PC. If it doesn't list the bus type, contact your dealer.

Different buses are characterized by size and speed, which are determined by the number of wires used to connect the PC's electrical components. In each expansion slot, for example, there are wires that connect the expansion card to the wires on the motherboard. The more wires, the faster the data is transferred.

Following is a list of some bus types found in PCs:

■ **ISA** (Industry Standard Architecture) bus slots transfer data at speeds of up to 16M per second. ISA expansion slots come in two sizes: full-size, or long slots; and half-height, or short slots.

■ **EISA** (Enhanced Industry Standard Architecture) bus slots transfer data at speeds of up to 32M per second. ISA cards can fit in EISA expansion slots, but they do not provide the EISA speed or features.

■ **MCA** (Micro Channel Architecture) bus slots transfer data at speeds of up to 40M per second. Neither ISA nor EISA cards can fit into MCA slots.

PART IV

Understanding Common PC Components

Understanding Keyboards

Before you can store data, or even process data, you must first input data. The most common device used for data input is the keyboard.

PC keyboards take their basic design straight from the familiar QWERTY typewriter layout—you will recognize the letter, number, and punctuation keys on the keyboard. They are very much like the ones found on a typewriter. However, the resemblance to a typewriter is only skin deep. The PC keyboard is easier and more forgiving to use than a typewriter. Don't be put off just because it has many more keys!

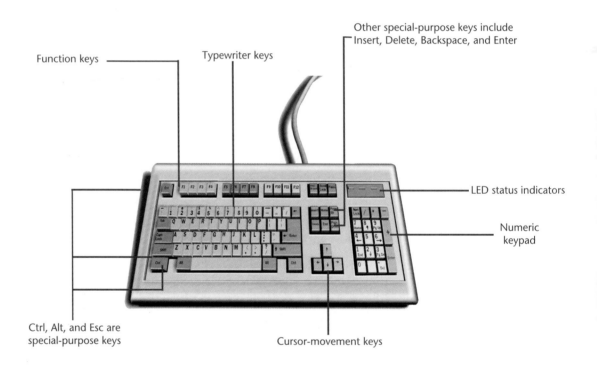

Function keys

Typewriter keys

Other special-purpose keys include Insert, Delete, Backspace, and Enter

LED status indicators

Numeric keypad

Ctrl, Alt, and Esc are special-purpose keys

Cursor-movement keys

The *typewriter (or alphanumeric)* keys let you type letters and numbers. When you press a key, you see the character on your monitor. The Tab, Caps Lock, Shift, and space bar perform the same functions as on a typewriter.

Function keys are labeled with the letter F and a number, for example, F1. Some keyboards have ten function keys; some keyboards have more. The function keys perform different tasks, depending on the software program you are using. In many programs, including Windows 95 and Microsoft Word, you can press the F1 function key to display a help screen.

The *cursor-movement keys* enable you to move around in a document or file displayed on the monitor. The arrow keys move the cursor up, down, left, or right. The PgUp (Page Up) and PgDn (Page Down) keys move, or *scroll*, the cursor one page at a time.

The *numeric keys* on the numeric keypad have two uses: the keys enable you to type numbers and to move around in your document or file (each number key corresponds to a cursor-movement key). The function of the keys depends on whether your keyboard's Num Lock status light is on or off. When the light is on, you can type the numbers; when it is off, you can use the keys for cursor-movement. You can turn the light on or off by pressing the Num Lock key at the top of the keypad. People accustomed to calculators or adding machines find it easier to enter numbers using the numeric keypad rather than the number keys at the top of the typewriter keyboard.

Special-purpose keys perform functions unique to computers. For example, you can use Backspace, Delete (Del), and Insert (Ins) keys to control the cursor and text on the monitor. Some other commonly used special-purpose keys are Enter, Escape (Esc), Alternate (Alt), and Control (Ctrl). You can use Enter like a carriage return to move the cursor to the next line, or, in some programs, to enter commands. The Esc key enables you to cancel the current activity in most software programs. In Windows 95, for example, pressing Esc clears a menu from the screen. The Alt and Ctrl keys, in combination with other keys, perform many functions. For example, pressing Ctrl, Alt, and Delete at the same time resets, or reboots, a PC.

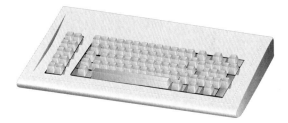

The first AT-model keyboard had 84 keys

> **NOTE** ▼
>
> *Regular touch keyboards* click when you press a key. *Soft touch keyboards* press down more easily and make very little noise. Try testing both kinds before you decide which feels right for you.

The *LED status indicators* show you if a keyboard function is on or off. For example, if the Caps Lock light is on, the keys you press appear as uppercase.

Not all keyboards look the same or have the same keys. The 101-key extended keyboard is the most popular for desktop PCs, but you may have a different version. The first AT-model keyboard had 84 keys. A 101-key enhanced keyboard was introduced with AT-model PCs.

A 101-key enhanced keyboard was introduced with AT-model PCs, and is sometimes called an AT keyboard

Keyboards designed for portable computers must fit in a small space. Some use different layouts, and some have fewer keys. Most portables do not have a separate numeric keypad.

A natural keyboard

Ergonomics, the science of designing equipment to avoid injuries and increase comfort, is a new trend in keyboard design. Some manufacturers make keyboards that don't look anything like a typewriter—the keyboards are curved or split into two independent sides which you can move and adjust anyway you choose. Also, the keys may be in a different order. The design of these ergonomic keyboards induces less stress on the wrists, hands, and arms of typists.

Understanding Mice

A mouse, like a keyboard, is an input device that you use to give information to the computer. The mouse can be easier to use than a keyboard because you don't have to remember commands or key combinations; you simply point at an object or command on-screen and press a button on the mouse to make a selection. Most software programs today are designed with the mouse in mind. Although you can get by with just a keyboard, it is much easier and more fun if you have a mouse.

> **NOTE** ▼
>
> You don't have to choose exclusively between a keyboard and a mouse. You may find that many programs are easiest to use when you combine the two.

The Anatomy of a Mouse

Although mice come in different shapes and sizes, all fit easily into the palm of your hand. When you hold the mouse correctly, your pointer finger sits gently on top of the left button. Your other fingers can rest on the other buttons, or guide the mouse around the desktop.

Cable

Buttons

Most mice have either two or three buttons. Most software programs use the left button to perform common functions, and the right button or middle button for special purposes. Your mouse may have only one button. Don't worry—you still can use it for most actions. A mouse gets its name from its shape. Notice that the cable that connects the mouse to the system unit looks like a tail.

On the underside of the mouse is a tracking ball, which translates the mouse movements into input signals that the PC can understand.

> **NOTE** ▼
>
> A *mouse pad* is a rubber pad that provides a uniform surface for the mouse to glide on. Your desk may work just fine, but often a mouse pad adds a bit of traction that makes the mouse easier to point.

Using a Mouse

To use a mouse, you need the following:

- A mouse

- A software application designed for use with a mouse, such as Windows or WordPerfect 6

- Software—called a *device driver* or *mouse driver*—that tells the PC how to use the mouse

- An open port or an expansion slot for connecting a mouse

- A mouse pad (optional)

You attach the mouse to a port on the PC with a cable. A *serial mouse* connects directly to a serial port that is built into the system unit of most computers. A *bus mouse* connects to a special mouse port and may require an adapter card that plugs into an expansion slot. Both types of mice basically look and act alike.

In addition, the PC must have a mouse device driver software program to tell the PC the type of mouse it is and the type of signals the mouse uses. The software driver may come already installed on your PC, or you may have to install it using a diskette that comes with the mouse.

Software programs designed for use with a mouse display a *mouse pointer* on-screen. The pointer may be an arrow, a small rectangle, an I-beam, or even a hand with a pointed finger. The pointer moves on-screen when you move the mouse. In some programs, the

Tracking ball

pointer changes to indicate the current action. For example, an arrow can change to an I-beam to indicate that the current action is entering text.

When you use a mouse, your position on-screen is indicated with one of these pointers (or something similar), depending on the program you're using and the action you're performing

Mouse Terminology

Term	Definition
Point	Move the pointer to the desired spot on the screen
Click	Press and release the left mouse button
Double-click	Press and release the left mouse button twice, as quickly as possible
Drag	Press and hold the left mouse button, while moving the pointer to another location
Drop	Release the mouse button after dragging
Point-and-shoot	Point, then click

A trackball on a laptop computer

To move the pointer, you gently slide the mouse around your desk or mouse pad. When you slide the mouse left, the pointer moves left. When you slide the mouse toward the back of your desk, the pointer moves toward the top of the screen. Sometimes you need to move the mouse without moving the pointer. For example, if you're sliding the mouse too close to the edge of the desk, but want to keep going in that direction, just pick up the mouse, move it back on the desk, and continue.

If you are left-handed, you may find the mouse awkward to use. Luckily, most software programs (including Windows 3.11 and Windows 95) and many mouse drivers enable you to reverse the mouse buttons so that you can use the right button to perform most functions and the left or middle buttons for special purposes. Check the documentation or the on-line help program to find out how.

NOTE ▼

If a software program does not display a pointer on-screen, it may not be designed for use with a mouse. Or, you may not have installed the mouse device driver correctly. Check the instructions that came with the mouse for more information or for a telephone number you can call for support.

Other Input Devices

A *trackball* looks like an upside-down mouse, and functions like a mouse to move a pointer around the screen. Instead of sliding it around a desktop or mouse pad, you rotate the trackball with your fingertips. Trackballs fit in small spaces, and often replace the mouse on portable PCs.

A *joystick* is a pointing device often used with games that benefit from realistic interaction. A flight simulator, for example, is more lifelike if you use a joystick to control it instead of a keyboard. Joysticks connect to a game port on the system unit.

A *scanner* enables you to input information that is on a piece of paper directly to the PC. Once you scan the information into the PC, you can use it as you use any file, which means that you can display it on a monitor, print it, and so on. You can scan pictures as well as text, but if you want to edit or display scanned pictures, your PC and monitor must be able to display graphics (see "Video Display Adapters" later in this part). In addition, scanners require special software. For example, to edit scanned text, you may need optical character recognition (OCR) software.

Joystick

Flatbed scanners are similar to copy machines, but instead of copying the information on the page to another piece of paper, the scanner translates the information into signals that the computer stores as a file. *Handheld scanners* work just like flatbed scanners, but you drag handheld scanners across the page of information.

An exciting area that is developing in PC input is voice-recognition. Already there are computers that have built-in devices that enable you to input information into PCs just by talking. In addition, some computers have pen devices that enable you to input information by writing on a digitizer or tablet.

Understanding Monitors

The *monitor* shows you the information you exchange with the computer. As you input information, the monitor displays it. As the PC processes the information and responds, the monitor displays the output. Virtually all the time you spend using your PC, you are looking at something displayed on a monitor.

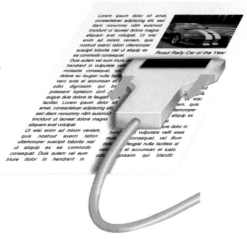

Monitors are either *monochrome* or *color*. Monochrome monitors display only two colors, usually black and white, amber and black, or green and black. Color monitors display anywhere from 16 colors to 16.7 million colors. Today, consumers usually buy PCs with color monitors. which are easier and nicer to look at than monochrome monitors, because most software developers design applications with color.

You measure the size of the monitor screen like a TV screen: diagonally, in inches. 14- or 15- inch screens are the standard for desktop PCs. Portables have smaller screens. If you use the PC to display graphics, such as for desktop publishing, you may want a monitor with a larger screen.

Monitors have *control knobs* that you use to adjust brightness, contrast, and the position of the information on-screen.

Screen

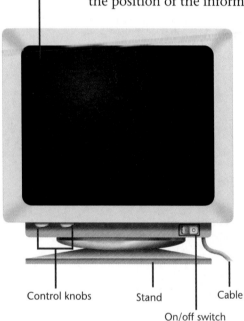

Control knobs   Stand   Cable

On/off switch

The monitor sits on a *stand*. A tilt-and-swivel stand lets you adjust the monitor to the position most comfortable for you.

A monitor has two *cables:* one connects it to the video adapter port on the system unit; the other plugs it into a regular electrical outlet.

A Word about Resolution

A monitor's resolution determines how detailed an image appears on-screen. Resolution is usually described in terms of the number of horizontal and vertical pixels that the monitor can display. *Pixel* is short for *picture element*. Each pixel is a dot on-screen; everything you see on-screen is made up of hundreds of thousands of tiny pixels.

NOTE ▼

The words *monitor*, *screen*, and *display* are used interchangeably.

Resolution is usually written as an equation, like this: horizontal pixels × vertical pixels. The more pixels, the higher the resolution. Higher resolution produces a sharper quality image on your display. So, a monitor that displays graphics in 800 × 600 resolution displays a sharper quality image than a monitor with 640 × 480 resolution. For the clearest image, you should look for 640 × 480 on 14" monitors, 800 × 600 on 15" monitors, and 1024 × 768 on 17-21" monitors

Sometimes resolution is described in terms of the monitor's dot pitch, instead of in terms of the number of pixels. The *dot pitch* is the distance from one pixel to the next pixel. The closer the pixels, the better the resolution, so the lower the dot pitch, the higher the resolution. Typical PC monitors have dot pitches ranging anywhere from .42 mm (low resolution) to .26 mm (high resolution).

You can easily display a low-resolution image on a high-resolution monitor (although it will still be a low-resolution image and will appear less sharp than a high-resolution image), but not vice versa. If you try to display a high-resolution picture on a low-resolution monitor, the picture will not be very clear.

Video Display Adapters

To display any kind of information, a monitor needs a *video display adapter*. The video display adapter is an expansion card that translates the signals the CPU processes into a format that the monitor can display. Usually, the video display adapter is built right into the motherboard, but sometimes it is an expansion card that fits in one of the motherboard's expansion slot. The video display adapter and the monitor must be compatible for images to display correctly.

The video display adapter controls the monitor's resolution, the number of colors it can display, and how fast images appear on-screen. In addition, video display adapters have their own memory chips for controlling how fast the monitor displays images. How fast the card can process the images determines how many colors it can display. Video display adapters have anywhere from 256K of memory, which easily supports 16 colors, to 1M or more, which can support up to 16.7 million colors at 640 × 480 resolution.

Video Display Adapters

Type	Description
Monochrome Display Adapter(MDA)	MDA cards control the display of monochrome monitors. They do not support color, and are virtually obsolete.
Color Graphics Adapter (CGA)	CGA cards regulate either monochrome or color monitors. They support a 25-row, 80-column text mode, and can display 4 colors from a palette of 16. These, too, are virtually obsolete.
Enhanced Graphics Adapter (EGA)	EGA cards also regulate either monochrome or color monitors. In text mode,EGA cards display 25 or 43 rows of text. In graphics mode, EGA cards support the CGA resolution as well as a 640 × 350 16-color mode.
Multi-Color Graphics Array (MCGA)	MCGA cards control the monitors of IBM's PS/2 models 25 and 30. They support the same modes as EGA cards, as well as a 640 × 480 two-color mode and a 320 × 200 256-color mode.
Video Graphics Array (VGA)	VGA cards support most common video standards. They display up to 50 rows and 80 columns in text mode. In graphics mode, they support 640 × 480 with 16 colors and 320 × 200 with 256 colors.
Super Video Graphics Array (SVGA)	SVGA cards are currently the standard.Typically, they add an 800 × 600 graphics mode and a 1024 × 768 graphics mode to the VGA capabilities, although with the correct device drivers you can use SVGA to display up to 1024 × 760, 1280 × 1024, and 1600 × 1200. If you plan to run graphics and multimedia applications, you should have an SVGA card.

When buying a monitor, as with other hardware devices, you should get the best quality you can afford. Even if you think you don't need a color monitor with an SVGA adapter, you might want those capabilities later.

Here are some of the things you should consider when selecting a monitor and display adapter:

■ *Color or monochrome.* Most software developers design applications for use on color monitors, and color is nicer to look at for long periods of time. If you will be using your computer for graphics, or desktop publishing, you will definitely want a color monitor.

■ *Resolution.* The types of software you use will dictate the resolution quality you need. Text-based applications, such as word processing, don't require as high a resolution as graphics-based applications, such as desktop publishing.

■ *Compatibility.* There are two issues related to compatibility: your software must be compatible with the monitor and display adapter type, and your monitor and video display adapter must be compatible with each other. If you have software, check to make sure that it can work with a new adapter. If you are changing just your monitor, or just the video adapter card, make sure the new component is compatible with the old.

■ *Monitor size.* 14-inch monitors are suitable for most home and business applications, but some applications, such as desktop publishing, are easier to use on a larger monitor.

■ *Video memory.* If the software you plan to run requires a large number of colors, you should consider a video display adapter card that comes with at least 2M of video RAM.

Understanding Printers

After you put information into the PC, you will probably want to get it out. A printer enables you to output (print) the information stored in your PC onto paper. However, there are so many different kinds of printers, all with different capabilities, that it can be hard to decide which kind is best for you.

Printers fall into two basic categories: *impact* and *non-impact*. In general, impact printers are noisier and have a poorer output quality than non-impact printers. They are also less expensive than non-impact printers. Impact printers print on continuous-feed, multipart, or cut-sheet paper, while non-impact printers typically print only on cut-sheet paper.

Impact Printers (Dot-Matrix)

Impact printers are similar to typewriters. They use a print head to strike a ribbon against paper, leaving the image of a character. The most common type of impact printer is the *dot-matrix printer*, which forms characters out of a series of dots.

Dot-matrix printers usually print about 150 to 300 characters per second.

Non-Impact Printers (Laser and Inkjet)

Non-impact printers use different methods to adhere ink or *toner* (ink powder) to the paper. Two common types of non-impact printers are *laser printers*, which combine a magnetic roller with toner to form characters or images on a page, and *inkjet printers*, which spray ink through holes in a matrix.

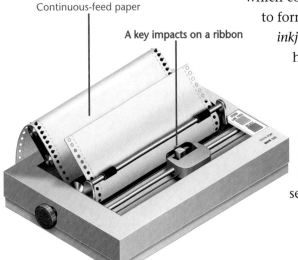

Continuous-feed paper

A key impacts on a ribbon

Laser printers are similar to copy machines, and can print at speeds ranging from 4 to 20 pages per minute. Inkjet printers can print about 120 to 240 characters per second, or 2 pages per minute.

A Word about Printer Languages

Printer languages are the software programs that control the printer. Three common printer languages are *PostScript*, *GDI*, and *Print Control Language (PCL)*.

PostScript is the name of a printer language that has become a standard for graphics printing with laser printers. Printers that use PostScript are simply called PostScript printers. Many programs support PostScript printing. PostScript printers usually cost more than other laser printers, but if you do a lot of graphics printing or need to share files with other users, a PostScript printer is worth the price; also, you can upgrade many printers to support the PostScript language.

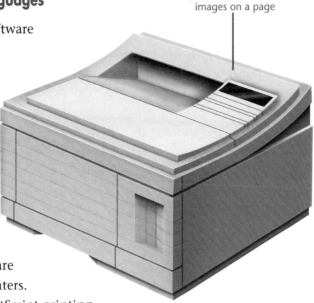

Laser printers use toner to form images on a page

NOTE ▼

Don't confuse printer *languages* with printer *drivers*. The drivers are the software programs that allow the PC to communicate with the printer. The printer languages are the software programs that control the printer itself.

PCL and GDI printers output documents at resolutions and speeds similar to PostScript printers, but they are not as common.

Considerations for Selecting a Printer

- *Speed*. Printer speed is rated by how many characters printers output in a second (abbreviated CPS) or how many pages printers output in a minute (abbreviated PPM). The higher the number, the faster the printer. The faster the printer, the less time you spend waiting for your documents to print.

- *Quality*. Quality is measured by how many dots per inch (DPI) the printer can print. The more dots per inch, the higher the resolution of the printed image. The higher the resolution, the better the quality. For impact printers, print quality is often described as *draft mode* (low resolution), *near-letter-quality mode* (medium resolution—often abbreviated NLQ), *letter-quality mode* (high resolution—abbreviated LQ), or *graphics mode* (high resolution). Laser printers typically offer 300 DPI or 600 DPI. Very high-quality printers can output at resolutions as high as 3,386 DPI. If you are outputting graphics, you want a high-resolution printer.

■ *Noise.* Some printers are noisier than others. Impact printers, for example, are louder than non-impact printers. You should decide how loud a printer you want to put into your office environment. However, if you cannot afford a quiet printer, you can purchase a box that you place over the printer to help cover the noise.

■ *Software support.* PCs communicate with printers using software programs called printer drivers, and some printers come with built-in printer languages, such as PostScript. You should make sure that the software programs you use support the printer driver and printer language for the printer you purchase.

■ *Paper, ink, and so on.* Consumables are the parts of the printer that must be replaced periodically in order to keep the printer working. For instance, printer ribbons, ink cartridges, and toner are all consumables. Different types of printers use different consumables. You should consider the cost of the consumables as well as how easy it is to change or replace them.

■ *Available fonts.* A font is a specific style of character that your PC displays or prints. Some printers come with built-in fonts, some let you use fonts stored on your PC, and some let you insert cartridges containing fonts directly into the printer. To find out which fonts your printer supports, check your printer manual.

■ *Other features.* Some printers come with options such as color or extra-wide carriage widths for printing on wide paper.

What Is a Multimedia Computer?

The newest trend in personal computing is *multimedia*. Multimedia is the ability to generate full-motion video and stereo sound on your PC, in addition to the traditional text and graphics. Multimedia is continually developing in terms of applications and technology, but already it is turning desktop PCs into video arcades, rock bands, and travel guides.

If you want to add the excitement of sound and motion to your PC, you should consider purchasing a system designed specifically for multimedia applications. Although theoretically you can use any PC for multimedia applications, in reality you should have at least the following:

Speakers

CD-ROMs

Headphones

CD-ROM drive

■ A fast 486- or Pentium-based computer with at least 256K byte of cache memory

■ 8M of RAM, although 16M is preferable

■ A high-quality video display with an SVGA graphics/video adapter card

■ A 16-bit sound card

■ A quad-speed CD-ROM drive

■ External speakers

■ A 500M hard drive

CD-ROMs and Multimedia

REVENGE OF THE MARTIANS

FROM VENUS

COPYRIGHT 1994 MSB INC.

Most multimedia software is available only on CD-ROM. That's because CD-ROMs can store a lot of information and music, animation, and video take up a lot of storage space. Some PCs come with a built-in CD-ROM drive, or you can attach a CD-ROM externally to a SCSI port on the system unit. In order for your PC to control the CD-ROM drive, you need to install the correct software device driver, which usually comes with the drive.

Some of the things you should look for when purchasing a CD-ROM drive for multimedia applications include:

■ *Speed.* CD-ROM drives tend to be slow. You should get a quad-speed drive if you can afford one, but at a minimum get a double-speed drive.

■ *Internal or External.* If you have room inside your PC, buy an internal CD-ROM drive. Internal drives take up less space on the desktop, and mean fewer cables hanging off the back of the system unit.

■ *Ease of Use.* Some CD-ROM drives have motorized trays that slide the disc in automatically; others are not motorized, so you must push the tray into the drive manually. Some drives require you to insert the disc in a *disc caddy* before inserting it into the drive.

■ *Compatibility.* Currently, standards are just beginning to develop in the multimedia arena, which means that there are lots of compatibility problems. You have to make sure that the CD-ROM drive is compatible with your PC and your sound card. You also need to be sure that the CD-ROMs you purchase are compatible with the CD-ROM drive you own. Check the format and system requirement information on the CD-ROM package to make sure you are buying an item that is compatible with the devices you have in your PC.

Sound Cards

For complete multimedia performance, you need a *sound card*. A sound card, which plugs into an expansion slot, enables the computer to make more noise. In addition to the beeps and alarms that all computers can make, a PC equipped with a sound card can generate high-quality sound effects and music. Without a sound card, you have to use headphones to hear the sounds made by your CDs.

Sound cards translate the digitized software signals into sounds that speakers can transmit. Sound cards enable you to hear digitized sound effects, such as an engine's roar, as well as the music from your favorite CDs. You can use some sound cards to record sounds and imitate speech.

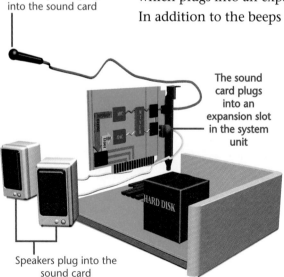

The microphone plugs into the sound card

The sound card plugs into an expansion slot in the system unit

HARD DISK

Speakers plug into the sound card

You can also use sound cards to physically connect your PC to microphones, speakers, and instruments that are compatible with the Musical Instrument Digital Interface (MIDI) standard. That way, you can compose and play back music on your PC.

> **NOTE** ▼
>
> If you want to record and compose music using your PC, you need to connect a MIDI (musical instrument digital interface) device to the MIDI input port on your sound card. With the appropriate software, you can record, edit, and mix music clips using your computer.

In order to use a sound card, you must have the correct software device driver. Windows comes with sound device drivers, as do many multimedia applications.

Two things to consider when purchasing a sound card include:

- *Quality.* If you want to generate high-quality music, you need a higher quality sound card than if you just want to generate sound-effects. 16-bit cards are better than 8-bit cards.

- *Compatibility.* Not all software is compatible with every sound card. Get a Creative Labs SoundBlaster or Media Vision card or one that is compatible with them.

Speakers

In order to hear the sound generated by the sound card on your PC, you need speakers. Without speakers, you need to use a headset to hear the sound coming from your PC.

Some things to think about when buying speakers include:

- *Quality.* High-fidelity amplified 100-watt stereo speakers produce the best quality sound. You can even purchase a sub-woofer to improve the depth of the sound and add impact.

- *Ease of use.* Make sure the volume control is conveniently located. Also, check to see if the speakers run on batteries or come with a plug for connecting them to an electrical wall outlet. If they run on batteries, make sure you can turn them off easily, or you'll soon run out of power.

- *Size.* You should determine the best size for your applications, taking into consideration the size of the room and the desktop area you are working on. If the speakers are large, make sure they are shielded, so that the magnets in the speakers won't interfere with the quality of the monitor display.

In case you've been living in the Biosphere for a few years, online services are commercial companies that provide you with access to information via telephone lines —for a fee. You use your computer and modem to call the company; then, the company connects you to the information you want.

Bulletin boards are central computers that you can also access using your PC and modem, usually paying only the telephone charges. BBSs are generally public message centers that you call in order to post messages or upload files that anyone can read. In return, you can download messages or information that other people have posted. BBSs are commonly established by groups and organizations to provide a local forum for exchanging ideas about a common topic.

The Internet is a world-wide communications system comprised of millions of computers linked together in a vast network. You gain access to the Internet via on-line services and Internet access services.

For more information about using communications to get online, see the section "The Internet" in Part VIII.

What You Need to Know about Communications

Communications is another of the most popular and fastest growing uses for PCs. If your PC is equipped for communications, you can easily exchange information and ideas with other PC users, either directly, over telephone lines, or indirectly, via online services (such as CompuServe, America Online, Prodigy, and Microsoft Network), electronic bulletin boards, or the Internet.

To use your PC for communications, you need:

- A telephone jack and telephone line

- A modem

- Communications software

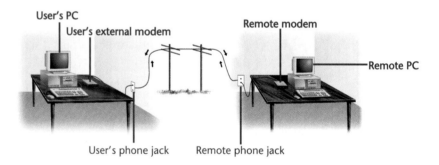

User's PC
User's external modem
Remote modem
Remote PC
User's phone jack
Remote phone jack

Modems

Modem is short for *MOdulator-DEModulator*. A modem enables a PC to connect to another PC, using a plain telephone line. After the PCs connect, you can transfer files or input any data that the other PC can output. You can use a modem to connect to an on-line service such as CompuServe or America Online, to check your office e-mail from home or from a vacation spot, or to connect to an office if you work at home provided you have the proper software. See the section "Communications Software" later in this part.

A modem sends data by translating the signals it receives from the CPU into signals that the telephone line can transmit. It receives data by translating the signals from the telephone line back into signals that the CPU can use.

There are two basic kinds of modems, *external* and *internal*. If you have an external modem, it connects to the PC via a cable to a serial port. The modem has two telephone jacks: one connects the modem to the telephone line and the other connects the modem to a telephone. The modem also plugs into an electrical outlet. You must turn on the modem before you use it to call another computer. If you have an internal modem, it attaches to an expansion slot on the motherboard in your PC. The modem draws power from the expansion slot, so it is on whenever the PC is on. On the back of the system unit are the telephone jack-like ports that let you attach a telephone and a telephone line to the modem.

An external modem

Phone jack

Internal modem card

NOTE ▼

You can attach a telephone to either kind of modem so you can make regular telephone calls on the same line that the modem uses when you are not using the modem.

Using Fax/Modems

Nowadays, no self-respecting office is without a facsimile (fax) machine. If you want the capability to send and receive faxes, without buying and maintaining a separate piece of equipment, you might consider making sure the modem you purchase has fax capabilities.

A *fax/modem* is an internal modem card or an external modem device that provides you with fax capabilities. If you have a fax/modem and the necessary software, you can transmit files from your PC to a fax machine, and you can receive data from a fax machine to save as a file on your PC.

The only drawback to a fax/modem is that you cannot transmit data from a printed page—you can only transmit data that is stored in a file on your PC. The transfer doesn't happen directly like it does on a fax machine: a fax/modem translates data into a graphic format file before sending it.

Communications Speed

A modem's speed, called *baud rate*, is measured in bits per second (bps or bit/sec). Speeds range from 300 bps to 28.8K bps. The higher the number, the faster the modem transmits the data. Although you can still get by with a 2400 bps, 4800 bps, or 9600 bps modem, if you plan to transmit or download information, you'll want a modem that supports at least a 14.4K bps transfer rate—the faster you send data, the lower your long-distance phone bill will be.

Some modems can compress data before transmitting it. Data compression actually shrinks the size of the signals so the modem can transmit the signals faster. Two common types of compression are MNP 5, which doubles transmission speed, and CCITT V.42bis, which quadruples transmission speed.

In addition, modems use one of three transmission standards:

V.22bis	Maximum transmission speed: 2.4K bps
V.32	Maximum transmission speed: 9K bps
V.32bis	Maximum transmission speed: 14.4K bps
V.34	Maximum transmission speed: 28.8K bps

Fall-back speed is a slower speed that the modem can use if the telephone lines, or the modem on the other end, can't transmit at the faster speed. Faster transmission is desirable for two reasons: you don't spend as much time waiting, and, because you usually pay telephone charges, the transmission costs less.

Communications Software

To use a modem, you must have a communications software program. Many different programs are available, including PC-Talk, Cross-Talk, and HyperTerminal. Don't confuse communications software with an on-line service or the Internet! An on-line service is a facility that allows you to connect to other computers. You need communications software in order to connect to the on-line service in the first place! See the sections "Communications" and "The Internet" in Part VIII for more information.

Most communications programs have features for storing telephone numbers as well as for automatic dialing and answering. Making a call with a modem is just like making a call with a telephone. You use the communications program to tell the computer what number to dial when it hears a dial tone, and, at the end of the call, you use the communications program to tell the computer to hang up.

You also use the communications program to set communications parameters, which are the rules the modem uses to make the call, and transmit the data. Communications parameters include:

NOTE ▼

If you are calling long distance, you must remember to tell the computer to dial 1 and the area code first. Some communications programs even make provisions for time delays when entering calling card numbers!

- The *transmission speed*, commonly 9600 bps or higher

- The *transfer protocol* that helps to make sure the data the modem transfers is error-free. Common protocols include XMODEM, YMODEM, and ZMODEM.

- The *data format*, usually text for files that include simple ASCII characters, or binary for graphics files.

- The *compression standard*, if desired. Common communications compression standards include MNP 5 and CCITT V.42bis.

NOTE ▼

Both the transmitting and receiving computers must use the same communications parameters in order for the connection to be successful.

What You Need to Know about Networks

Personal computers were designed to be used by one person at a time, for one task at a time. That's why manufacturers named them personal computers. Today, many computers are still stand-alone systems, which means that the computers are self-sufficient units, standing alone on their desktops.

However, just as the world has grown into a so-called global village, and you live in a so-called wired society, you can connect, or wire, your PC to other PCs, linking you into groups called *networks*.

A connection between two or more computers is a network. PCs on a network can share data, applications, and peripherals (such as printers). Businesses find that by connecting computers into networks, productivity is increased and overhead is reduced. Everyone on the network uses the same tools and can communicate easily. Networks mean fewer expenditures for costly resources, such as printers, and can protect important data by instituting company-wide policies for security and file backups.

NOTE ▼

You've probably heard about the mother of all networks: the Internet. The Internet is a worldwide communications system made up of tens of millions of computers linked together. You'll learn more about the Internet in Part VIII, "Using Your Computer."

Kinds of Networks

There are two basic kinds of networks: *local area networks (LANs)* and *wide area networks (WANs)*. LANs usually are smaller than WANs, linking only one building, or even one department. WANs cover more territory, linking several buildings, even in different cities, states, or countries.

LANs can be connected to each other, and to WANs, to increase the size of the network. A wide variety of networking and internetworking devices are available for connecting computers into networks and networks into larger networks.

Most LANs connect PCs to the network via cables and network adapter cards. Each computer on a network is called a *node*. Sometimes, computers on a network are called *workstations*, or *clients*.

A *server*, a more powerful PC, manages all the PCs on a LAN. The server stores the software programs and files that everyone shares, and it controls the flow of data. Security systems, such as assigned passwords, make sure that only the people who are supposed to access certain data can do so. A *network administrator* makes sure that the network is running smoothly and that everyone has access to the information they need.

Networks require special software in order to work. A network operating system controls the system functions of each PC, and requires applications that can run on networks.Two common network operating systems are Windows for Workgroups and Novell NetWare.

There are three basic types of LANs:

- In a *token-ring network*, nodes pass data from one node to another in a circular—or ring—pattern.

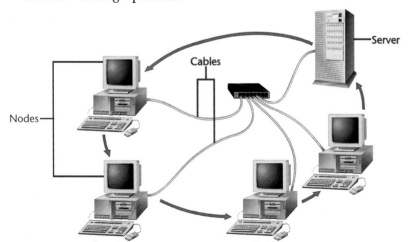

- In a *star network*, a central device, either a file server or a star controller, attaches each PC and peripheral directly to the network.

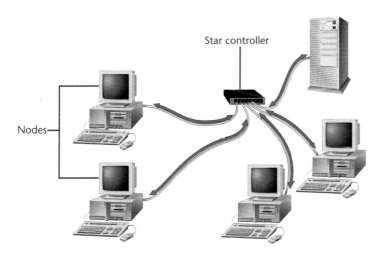

Star controller

Nodes—

- In a *bus network*, a cable, called a bus, attaches all PCs and peripherals to the network.

How Networks Affect Your Work

You may be connected to a PC network and not even know it. You still have a PC on your desk. The PC looks and acts the same as a PC not connected to a network. The difference is that you can communicate with other people on the network without using a modem.

On a network, you can easily send e-mail messages to other users, and you can participate in workgroups where you share the same data files for projects you are working on with other people on the network. Many applications are designed specifically for workgroups, including Lotus Notes, Windows 95, and Windows for Workgroups. On a network, you can be sure that everyone is using the most up-to-date information and programs.

A network operating system

A bus network

Another difference between networked PCs and stand-alone PCs is that some networked PCs do not have all of the basic system components. For example, because networked PCs share devices, some networked PCs may not have hard disk drives. These PCs must store files on floppy disks or on the file server. Also, networked PCs probably don't have individual printers because several PCs on the network share the same printer.

PART V
Understanding Your Operating System

What Is an Operating System?

An *operating system* is a group of software programs that provides the instructions you need to control your PC. Without an operating system, you would not be able communicate with your computer and your computer would not know how to communicate with you.

Think of an operating system as a general contractor at a building site. The general contractor makes sure that all other service providers—the electrician, the plasterer, the roofer—show up at the right time, do the job that's expected of them, and don't get in each other's way. The workers communicate with each other and with the homeowner through the general contractor, and the job gets done to the homeowner's specifications.

The operating system makes sure that all parts of the PC work together to get the job done, according to the specifications you enter as commands. The operating system controls the flow of input and output, and calls in the hardware and software to perform the necessary services at the right time.

Without an operating system, you would have to speak and understand the signals used by every piece of hardware connected to the PC. You would have to input instructions detailing every action you want the PC to perform, from how to load a program into memory to copying disks and printing files.

What Does the Operating System Do?

Some of the services provided by an operating system include:

- *Disk management.* The operating system helps you control your storage devices. For example, you can use the operating system to format, label, copy, and organize the information hard and floppy disks contain.

NOTE

Most PC manufacturers install an operating system on a PC's hard disk, but give the consumer the original program floppy disks for backup. Keep the disks in a safe place, in case you need them in the future.

- *File management.* The operating system helps you organize the files in which you store data. For example, the operating system keeps track of a file's location, name, size, and creation and edit dates. You can use the operating system to list all file information.

■ *Device management.* The operating system provides the instructions the computer needs to control peripherals such as keyboards, printers, mice, and modems. For example, the operating system interprets mouse movements and keystrokes into commands that the computer can understand.

■ *Program management.* The operating system provides the interface a software program needs to communicate with the PC. For example, the operating system controls the input and output between a word processing program and the keyboard, and a communications program and the modem.

■ *User management.* The operating system provides an easy-to-use interface that enables you to communicate with the PC in a language you understand. Because of the operating system, you do not need to know a cryptic programming language to start an application program. You can type a word in English, select a menu item, or click on an icon on the screen.

What's an Interface?

You and your PC do not speak the same language. It understands program code; you understand English. The operating system translates English into

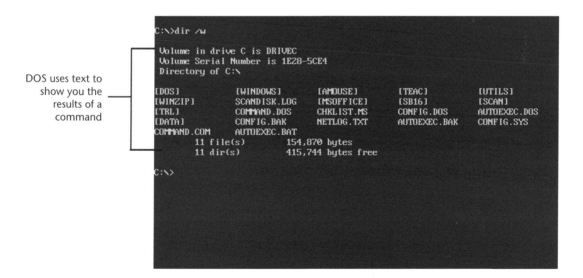

DOS uses text to show you the results of a command

```
C:\>dir /w

 Volume in drive C is DRIVEC
 Volume Serial Number is 1E28-5CE4
 Directory of C:\

[DOS]            [WINDOWS]        [AMOUSE]         [TEAC]           [UTILS]
[WINZIP]         SCANDISK.LOG     [MSOFFICE]       [SB16]           [SCAN]
[TRL]            COMMAND.DOS      CHKLIST.MS       CONFIG.DOS       AUTOEXEC.DOS
[DATA]           CONFIG.BAK       NETLOG.TXT       AUTOEXEC.BAK     CONFIG.SYS
COMMAND.COM      AUTOEXEC.BAT
        11 file(s)          154,870 bytes
        11 dir(s)           415,744 bytes free

C:\>
```

code, and code into English so that you can communicate with your PC. This point of communication is a *user interface*.

DOS, one of the most common PC operating systems, uses a *command-line interface*. You type the command you want, and DOS responds by executing it and displaying output on your screen. DOS is not considered *user-friendly*—in other words, it's not easy to use—because it involves a lot of cryptic commands and messages that you have to read and type.

Windows 95, the newest PC operating system, uses a *graphical user interface (GUI)*. You interact with the PC by using a mouse to choose items from menus, or to select pictures, called *icons*, that represent programs or parts of your computer.

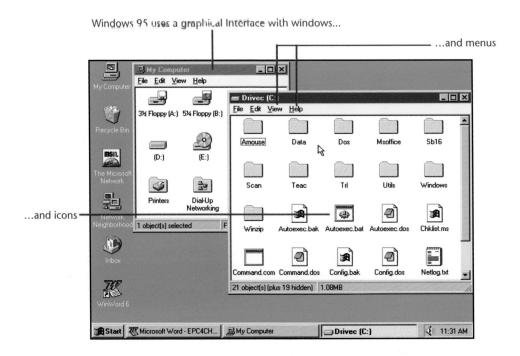

Windows 95 uses a graphical Interface with windows...

...and menus

...and icons

Windows 3.X, the previous version of Windows, which you may still be using, also uses a GUI. However, technically speaking, Windows 3.X is an *operating environment*, not an operating system. Windows 3.X cannot work without the DOS operating system. Thus, if you use Windows 3.X, you get the benefits of the GUI, but you still have to follow a lot of cryptic DOS rules.

Windows 3.X also uses
a graphical interface

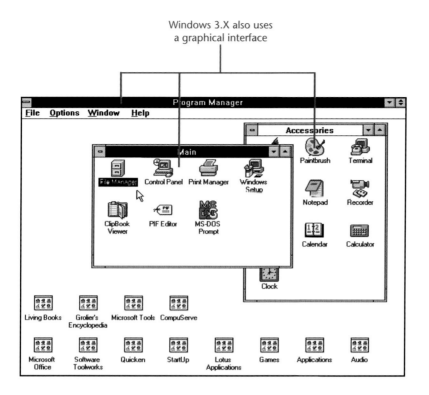

You may find that using a graphical interface is easier than using a command-based or text-based interface because you don't have to remember commands. That's why Windows is so popular.

Software Versions

Traditionally, software developers identified different versions of a software program with different numbers. Each time developers release a new version of a software program, it gets a new number.

If changes in a new version are minor, such as fixing a small problem, called a *bug*, only the number to the right of the decimal point changes. If the changes to the program are significant, such as adding lot of new features or completely rewriting the program, the number to the left of the decimal point changes.

For example, DOS version 1.0 was introduced along with the first PCs. Since then, DOS has been improved considerably, and the most current version of DOS is 6.22.

So how does Windows 95 fit in? Prior to Windows 95, the most current version of Windows was 3.11. However, because Windows 95 is a complete operating system that doesn't rely on DOS, it is very different from Windows 3.11, which cannot operate without DOS. So Microsoft gave Windows 95 an unprecedented identifier.

Sometimes in a software version number, an X replaces the number to the right of the decimal point, such as DOS 5.X. There isn't really a DOS version 5.X. The X means that whatever is said about the software is true for all of the versions of DOS since the major upgrade to DOS 5, but before the major upgrade to DOS 6. This list would include DOS 5.1, DOS 5.2, and so on.

Understanding Windows

Windows is based on the idea that the monitor screen is just like your desktop. In fact, in Windows, the screen is called the *desktop*.

Just as you can have more than one project on your desk at once, in Windows you can have more than one application open at once. When you have a job to do, you place all the documents, books, calculators, notebooks, and other accessories that you need within reach while you work. Similarly, in Windows, you can keep the files and tools you need to do a job available on-screen while you work.

Windows was originally designed to make it easy to use DOS. With Windows 3.X installed on your PC, you don't have to look at DOS or know much about DOS in order to use your applications, but DOS still runs the show.

NOTE

Although Windows 95 is different from Windows 3.X, it uses a lot of the same concepts, so if you use Windows 3.X, you will feel comfortable with Windows 95.

Windows 95, however, takes over the operating system functions of DOS. If you have Windows 95 installed on your PC, you don't need to even think about DOS. Everything you need to control your PC, your software, and your hardware is part of Windows 95. (Even in Windows 95, however, you can still get to the DOS prompt if you really want to. Just click the Start buttom, select Programs, and then select MS-DOS Prompt.)

All software applications designed for use with Windows have the same basic commands and screen elements as Windows—once you learn to use one Windows application, you can quickly learn to use all of the others. This is true for applications designed to run with Windows 3.X as well as those written to run with Windows 95.

Getting to Know Windows 95

Windows 95 is a very *intuitive* software program. In other words, it is designed to work the way you think it should work. For example, if you see the word Start on your screen, you can bet that's a good place to start something.

Windows 95 is a flexible program. The easiest way to use it is to click around in it with a mouse. You can click menu commands, program icons, shortcuts on the desktop, or buttons on a toolbar. Also, if you prefer, you can use a keyboard to accomplish all Windows 95 tasks.

Windows 95 comes set up for typical use, but you can customize it for your own convenience. For example, you can create shortcuts for accessing the programs you use most frequently and you can customize the appearance of the desktop. In Part VI, you learn how to perform some of the basic Windows 95 tasks.

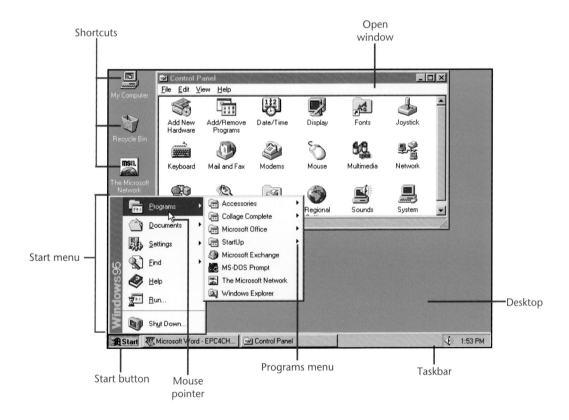

The Benefits of Windows 95

With Windows 95, you can do the following with a simple click of the mouse button:

■ *Start programs.* Rather than memorize and type commands to start a program, you point to the program you want and click the mouse button. The program opens on-screen in a window.

■ *Manage files.* You can use Windows 95 to perform file-management tasks. You can select commands from a menu rather than typing them and you can display files in a window on-screen. Displaying several windows of files at once makes it easier to copy, move, and rename files without making time-consuming mistakes.

■ *Accessorize.* Windows 95 comes with a slew of useful programs and features to help you get your work done faster and easier.

■ *Run multiple programs.* You can run more than one program at a time, switching between the programs and even exchanging data between programs.

■ *Use Windows 95 programs.* Although with Windows 95 you can use programs written for Windows 3.X or DOS, there are advantages to using applications written specifically for Windows 95. Not only do Windows 95 applications take advantage of Windows 95 features, but these applications are designed to look and work the same way as Windows 95, which means that once you learn the basic skills for using Windows 95, you know the basic skills for using all Windows 95 applications.

Of course, Windows 95 isn't the answer for everyone. For one thing, it requires tremendous computer resources to work efficiently. Without a Pentium or fast 486-based PC and 8M to 16M of RAM, you spend a lot of time waiting in front of the Windows 95 screen. If you already have Windows 3.X and a lot of Windows 3.X applications, you may not want to upgrade to Windows 95.

Some Things You Get with Windows 95

Windows 95 comes with a lot of built-in features that make it easy and fun to use your PC. It has features for controlling multimedia applications and communicating on a network. Following is a sampling of some of the "goodies" that you get with Windows 95:

Windows 95 Accessories

Accessory	Purpose
WordPad	Simple word processing and formatting
Paint	Create graphics
Media Player	Play multimedia applications
Sound Recorder	Play back and record sound
CD Player	Play music CDs in your computer's CD player
Calculator	Perform mathematical calculations
Microsoft Exchange	Send and receive electronic mail on a network
Microsoft Fax	Send and receive faxes
Recycle Bin	Hold deleted files until recovered or permanently deleted

What about DOS?

DOS, which stands for *disk operating system*, is still the most common PC operating system. Microsoft's version of DOS is MS-DOS. IBM's version of DOS is PC-DOS. The two operating systems are virtually the same and generally are referred to simply as DOS.

DOS has more than 100 commands you can use to control a PC. Most of these commands have names that indicate their functions. The COPY command, for example, enables you to copy files, and the FORMAT command enables you to format floppy disks. You probably use fewer than ten DOS commands frequently. Part VII, "DOS Tasks," covers some of the most useful DOS commands.

Typing Commands at the DOS Prompt

To get DOS to do something, you have enter a command. DOS identifies the line on your monitor where you can type commands by displaying a greater-than symbol (>). This is the *DOS command-line prompt*. You know that DOS is ready to process a command when you see the DOS prompt on your screen.

The DOS prompt ——
A command typed on
the DOS command line ——

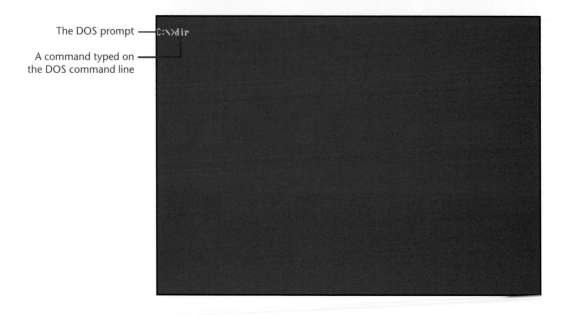

You type a command to the right of the DOS prompt and press the **Enter** key. DOS processes the command and displays the result.

DOS is particular about the way you type a command. If you don't type in the command according to its *syntax* (the rules that control the format of the command), DOS cannot process the command. You must type in the correct syntax of the command on the command line to execute the command; for example, if you leave a space between the prompt and the command, DOS does not recognize the command. When you press **Enter**, DOS responds with the message Bad command or file name. If you make a mistake typing a command, you can press the **Backspace** key to delete the mistake, then continue typing. If you press **Enter** before you notice the mistake, you can press **Esc** to try to stop the command before DOS tries to execute it.

For information about the correct names and syntax for all DOS commands, see Que's *Using MS-DOS 6, Special Edition*. For information about using common DOS commands, see Part VII, "DOS Tasks," later in this book.

Special DOS Files

Even if you use Windows 95, there are three special DOS files that you should know about: COMMAND.COM, CONFIG.SYS, and AUTOEXEC.BAT.

- *COMMAND.COM.* This file processes the DOS commands. When you enter a command into DOS, COMMAND.COM executes the appropriate functions.

- *CONFIG.SYS.* This DOS file contains commands. The CONFIG.SYS commands tell DOS if the peripherals or application programs need to be set up in a certain way. For example, CONFIG.SYS includes a command about how many files DOS must set aside to run programs. CONFIG.SYS also might include a command telling DOS how to allocate memory resources.

- *AUTOEXEC.BAT.* This file contains commands you want DOS to perform each time you start the computer. DOS always looks for the AUTOEXEC.BAT file when it starts, and executes all the commands it finds there. For example, AUTOEXEC.BAT might include the command for automatically starting a particular software application, or for opening a certain file every time you start the computer.

NOTE

You must be careful never to delete these three files. If you understand what you are doing, you can edit AUTOEXEC.BAT and CONFIG.SYS by opening them in a word processing program, but you should never try to change or move COMMAND.COM.

Other PC Operating Systems

Most PCs use DOS or Windows—or a combination of the two—but there are other operating systems available. Some of the other operating systems are compatible with DOS and Windows 3.X, which means they can control applications

NOTE

Currently, few operating systems run Windows 95 programs.

written for DOS or Windows 3.X. Some operating systems are not compatible with DOS and Windows 3.X, which means that you must use that particular operating system's applications. Trying to run a DOS program on a non-DOS operating system is like trying to play an eight-track tape in your cassette player, or a 45 RPM record at $33^1/_3$ RPM.

This table lists some other PC operating systems:

Other Operating Systems

Operating System	Compatible with DOS?
OS/2	Yes
DR DOS	Yes
Novell DOS	Yes
UNIX	No
Xenix	No
CP/M	No

Data Storage and Your Operating System

One task of the operating system is to store data. Storage devices, under the guidance of an operating system, use a multilevel filing system for keeping track of where the disk stores data. The organization is similar to the way office filing cabinets store paper files.

For example, instead of a file cabinet, a PC has a disk. Instead of file folders in the file cabinet, you separate information into electronic folders on the disk. Instead of putting paper documents in file folders in the file cabinet, you store electronic files in the electronic folders on the disk.

Understanding Folder Organization

In order to keep track of where your disk stores data, you have to understand folders. Disks do not come with folders already on them. When you format a disk, the operating system creates a main folder, called the *root*. You create additional folders as you need them (you'll learn how in Part VI, "Windows 95 Tasks"). Some programs automatically tell the operating system to create the folders the program needs during installation. You create folders in order to organize your data. For example, if you write a lot of letters with your PC, you could create a folder called Letters to store your letters. Anytime you need to find one of your letter files, you know to look in the Letters folder.

If you have so many letters that it is getting hard to find the one you need in the Letters folder, you can create subfolders within the folder. For example, you can create a Jobs subfolder and a Mom subfolder.

> **NOTE** ▼
>
> Until Windows 95, folders were called directories. A lot of people will continue calling them directories. When you hear someone refer to directories, they are talking about folders.

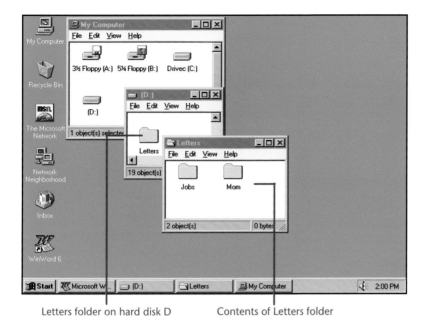

Letters folder on hard disk D   Contents of Letters folder

Naming Files and Folders

You create and name folders with your operating system, but you also create and name files when you work with an application program. For example, if you type a letter in WordPerfect, you save and assign a name to the letter through WordPerfect.

With DOS and Windows 3.X, you have to follow these strict rules for naming files and folders:

■ A name can contain up to eight characters.

■ A name can include the letters A through Z, the numbers 0 through 9, and the symbols !, @, #, $, %, ^, &, ( ), -, _ , and ~.

■ You can add a three-character extension to a file name (separated from the file name by a period). The extension usually indicates the type of file. For example, DOC files are document files, and BAK files are backup files.

■ No matter whether you use uppercase or lowercase letters, the file or folder name appears sometimes in all uppercase and sometimes in all lowercase.

Typical File Extensions

File extensions tell you what kind of files you are dealing with:

Extension	Meaning
BAK	Backup file
BAT	Batch file
COM	Program file
EXE	Program (executable file)

Some application programs are associated with certain file extensions:

Extension	Application
DOC	Microsoft Word
WK*	Lotus 1-2-3
XLS	Microsoft Excel
SAM	Ami Pro
BMP	Paint (or any application that uses bitmapped graphics format)

With Windows 95, you can name files and folders anything you want: your file name can be up to 256 characters long, you can use both uppercase and lowercase letters, and Windows 95 doesn't attach an extension.

DOS Folder or File Names and Windows 95 Folder or File Names

DOS Names	Windows 95 Names
YEREPS.DOC	Year-End Report Documents
TOMOM.LET	Letter to Mom
65MEMOS	Memos written on June 5th
95TAXES.WK4	1995 Tax Documents ready for auditing
95BUDGET	1995 Budget Plan
letbw121	Letter written to Bob White on December 1st

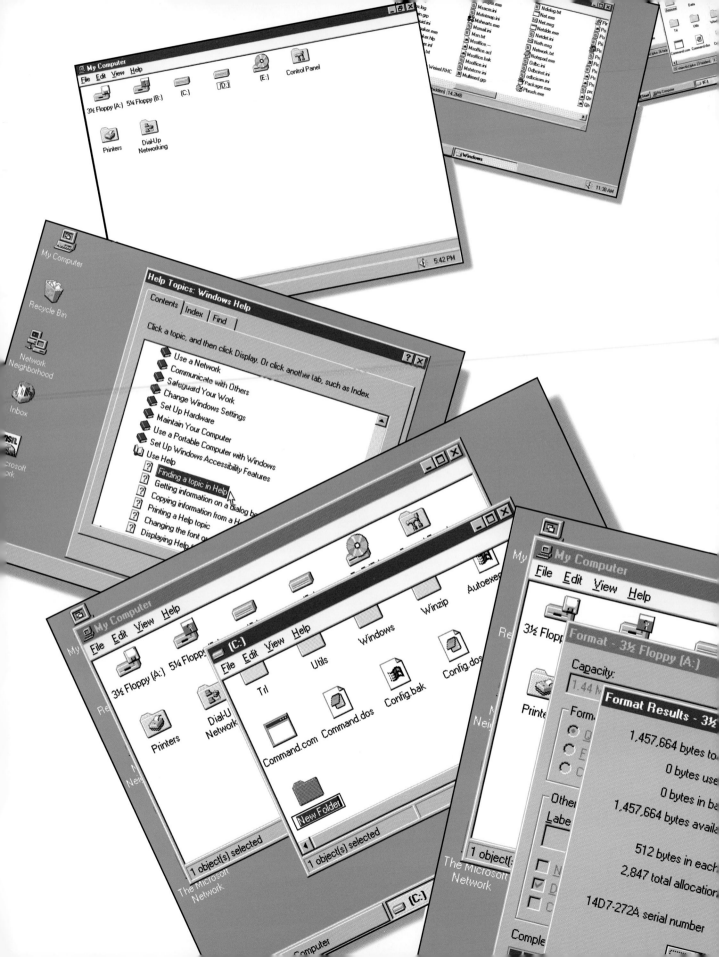

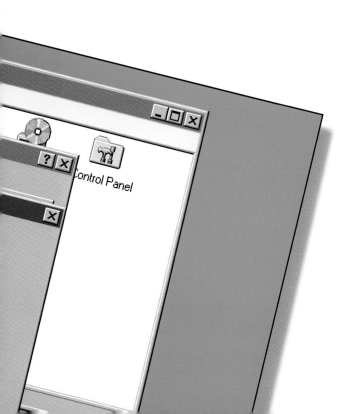

PART VI

Windows 95 Tasks

In this part, you learn how to use some of the basic features of Microsoft Windows 95. With Windows 95, you will find it easy to control your PC, application programs, and files. You do not need to remember how to type command syntax as you do in DOS; all you need to do is use your mouse to point and click.

Before you begin the tasks in Part VI, you must make sure that you have Windows 95 installed on your PC. (If it is installed, Windows 95 appears on your screen when you start your computer. If it is not installed, consult the Windows documentation for information about installation.) If you have a different version of Windows (such as Windows 3.1), you will not be able to follow the tasks in this chapter. For tasks that you can follow with an earlier version of Windows, see Que's *Easy Windows 3.11.*

Although you can use Windows 95 with just a keyboard, to really take advantage of the Windows interface, and to complete the tasks in this chapter, you need to use a mouse.

Windows 95 is a graphical user interface (GUI), which means you see on-screen graphical depictions of your computer system, programs, and files. Windows 95 displays messages and commands in plain English, not cryptic abbreviations or technical jargon. In addition, all Windows 95 application developers design programs around the same interface, so once you learn to use Windows 95, you can easily learn to use other Windows 95 applications.

Although Windows 95 uses plain English, it also has its own set of terms and concepts that you should understand before beginning:

■ *Windows* is both the name of the GUI program and the term used to identify rectangular boxes that appear on-screen to display information. Windows the program is always capitalized; lowercase "windows" refers to the rectangular areas on-screen.

■ The Windows 95 *desktop* is the whole screen that displays Windows 95. On the desktop, you open and arrange icons and windows in order to manage your files and programs.

■ The *active window* is the window in which you are currently working. You can open more than one window in Windows 95, but you can work in only the active window.

- You use the *mouse* to move the *mouse pointer* around the screen so that you can make choices and position the insertion point. Most of the time, the mouse pointer looks like an arrow, but sometimes it changes shape.

- The *insertion point* is a bar that appears on-screen at the location where you type information, such as in a text box within a dialog box.

- *Icons* are small pictures that represent application programs, groups of programs, directories, and files. On the Windows 95 desktop, icons also represent shortcuts, which you can use to quickly access a feature, program, or window.

- *Dialog boxes* are windows (note the lowercase w) where you enter additional information that Windows 95 (note the uppercase) needs to execute a command. In dialog boxes, you make choices by clicking *buttons*, *check boxes*, or *item names*, or by typing information in a *text box*.

- *Menus* are lists from which you choose commands. Each window has a main menu bar across the top of it. When you click a menu item name, the menu opens on-screen.

- The *Taskbar* appears at the bottom of the desktop. The names of all open windows appear as buttons on the Taskbar. You click a name to make that window active and display on-screen the program running within the window.

- The *Start button* is a button at the left corner of the Taskbar. You use it to open the Start menu, from which you start programs, get help, change settings, find files, or exit Windows 95.

- An *object* is an item on the Windows 95 desktop that you select, move, copy, open, or delete. Folders and files are objects, as are icons.

- The *Recycle Bin* is the folder where Windows 95 stores objects that you delete. As long as an object is in the Recycle Bin, you can recover it. When you empty the Recycle Bin (or, when it gets too full, Windows empties the bin), Windows 95 deletes the objects from the disk.

- The *Clipboard* is a temporary storage area where you keep a file, folder, piece of text, or a graphic until you need it. You use the Clipboard to move and copy objects from one place to another place. Using the Clipboard, you can move and copy objects as well as exchange data between different programs.

TASK 1

Starting and Shutting Down Microsoft Windows 95

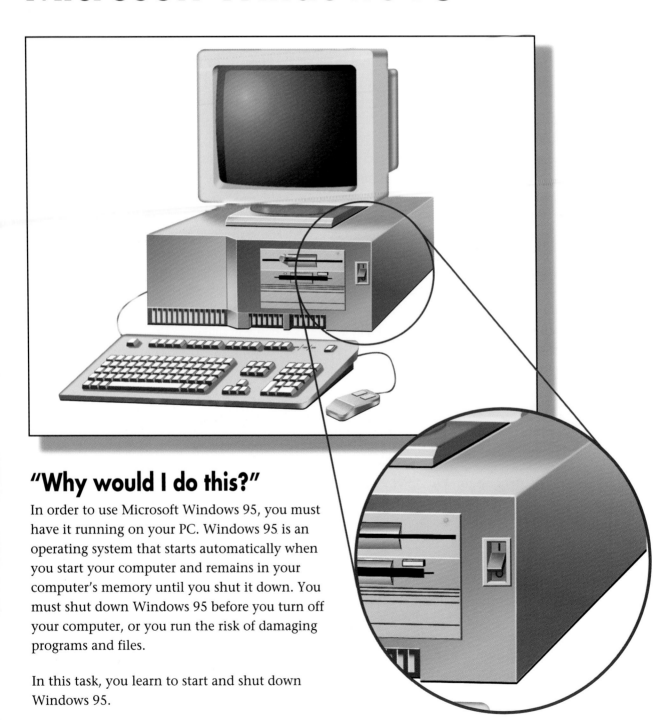

"Why would I do this?"

In order to use Microsoft Windows 95, you must have it running on your PC. Windows 95 is an operating system that starts automatically when you start your computer and remains in your computer's memory until you shut it down. You must shut down Windows 95 before you turn off your computer, or you run the risk of damaging programs and files.

In this task, you learn to start and shut down Windows 95.

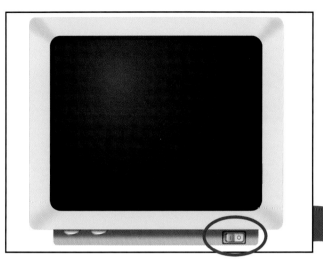

1 Press the **power switch** on your monitor into the on position. Look for the monitor's on/off switch under the screen, on the right side, or on the back.

2 Press the **power switch** on your computer's system unit into the on position. When the computer starts, you see a message or two flash on the screen, and Windows 95 begins loading into your computer's memory.

> **NOTE** ▼
>
> If you see the message Non-system disk or disk error, there is a disk in the floppy drive that does not contain the startup files. Remove the disk, and try starting Windows again.

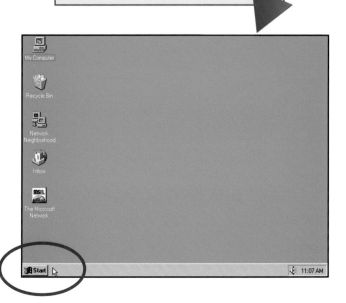

3 Click on the **Start** button on the Taskbar at the bottom of the Windows 95 desktop. The Start menu opens to display a list of programs and commands you can choose.

> **WHY WORRY?**
>
> The items on your Start menu may not be the same as the items on the Start menu in the illustrations in this part. You can change the Start menu to suit your own work habits.

4 To shut down your computer, click on **Shut Down** on the Start menu. Shut Down is the command you use to close Windows 95 and prepare to turn off your computer. This step displays a dialog box that asks if you are sure you want to shut down Windows 95.

NOTE ▼

To choose a command from a menu quickly with the keyboard, press the letter on the keyboard that corresponds with the one underlined in the command name.

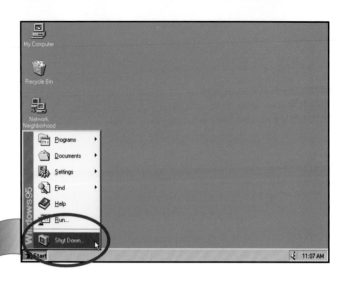

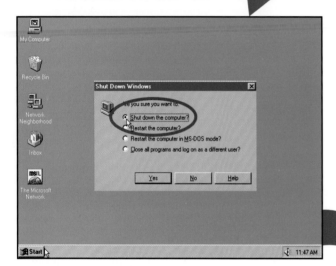

5 Select the **Shut down the computer?** option. This option tells Windows you are done working and want to turn off your computer.

WHY WORRY?

Your Windows 95 desktop may not look the same as the one in these illustrations. Someone may have changed the appearance of your desktop, or you may have different programs installed on your computer. Don't worry, no matter what your desktop looks like, you use the same steps to accomplish these tasks.

6 Click on **Yes**. Clicking Yes in the Shut Down Windows dialog box confirms that you want to shut down Windows and turn off your computer. Windows closes, and a message appears telling you that you can safely turn off your computer. ■

NOTE ▼

You use options in the Shut Down Windows dialog box to restart your computer in Windows 95 or to restart your computer in MS-DOS.

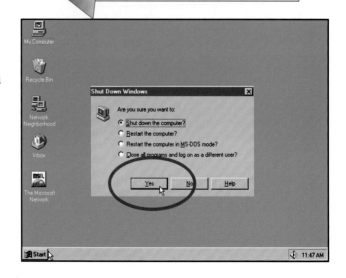

Opening, Switching, and Closing Windows

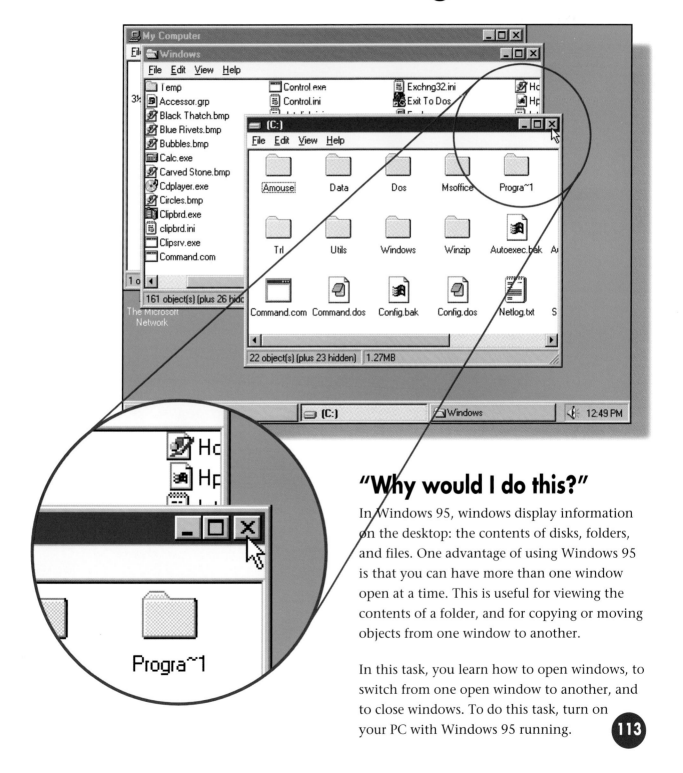

"Why would I do this?"

In Windows 95, windows display information on the desktop: the contents of disks, folders, and files. One advantage of using Windows 95 is that you can have more than one window open at a time. This is useful for viewing the contents of a folder, and for copying or moving objects from one window to another.

In this task, you learn how to open windows, to switch from one open window to another, and to close windows. To do this task, turn on your PC with Windows 95 running.

113

1 Double-click on the **My Computer** icon on the desktop. Double-clicking on My Computer opens the My Computer window. Icons in the My Computer window represent the components of your computer.

WHY WORRY?

If the window does not open, you probably did not double-click fast enough. Simply clicking on an icon once selects the icon, but does not open the window. Try double-clicking again.

2 Double-click on the drive icon labeled **[C:]**. This opens a window displaying the contents of your hard drive [C:]. Icons in this window represent the folders and files stored on drive [C:].

3 Double-click on the **Windows folder** in the drive [C:] window. This opens a window displaying the contents of the Windows folder. The window lists all of the folders and files in the Windows folders.

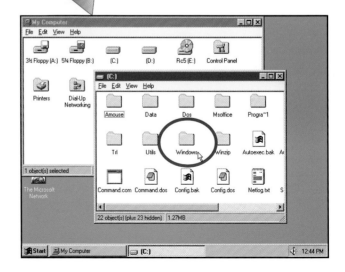

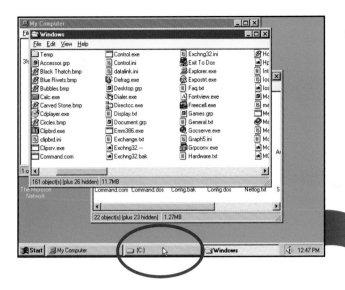

4 Click the drive **[C:]** button on the Taskbar at the bottom of the desktop. This makes the drive [C:] window *active*. The active window moves to the top of the desktop, and its title bar appears highlighted. Also, on the Taskbar, the button of the active window appears *depressed*.

5 Click the **Close** button in the upper right corner of the drive [C:] window. The Close button is the third of three buttons at the right end of the window's title bar. It has an X on it. This closes the drive [C:] window. Clicking the Close button in any window closes the window. The Windows window and the My Computer window are still open. ■

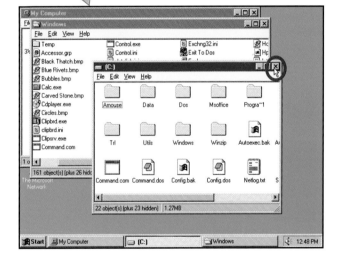

NOTE ▼

The file names in your folders may not display file name extensions (a dot and three letters following the file name). With the extensions displayed, you can identify files and what they are used for more easily. (To learn more about file extensions, see the section "Naming Files and Folders," in Part V.) To display file extensions in Windows 95, double-click the My Computer icon. Select Options from the View menu. Click on the View tab and remove the check mark from the Hide MS-DOS File Extensions for File Types that Are Registered check box.

NOTE ▼

You can also use menu commands to close a window. In the active window, click on the word File on the menu bar, and click on the Close command.

Moving, Resizing, and Scrolling Windows

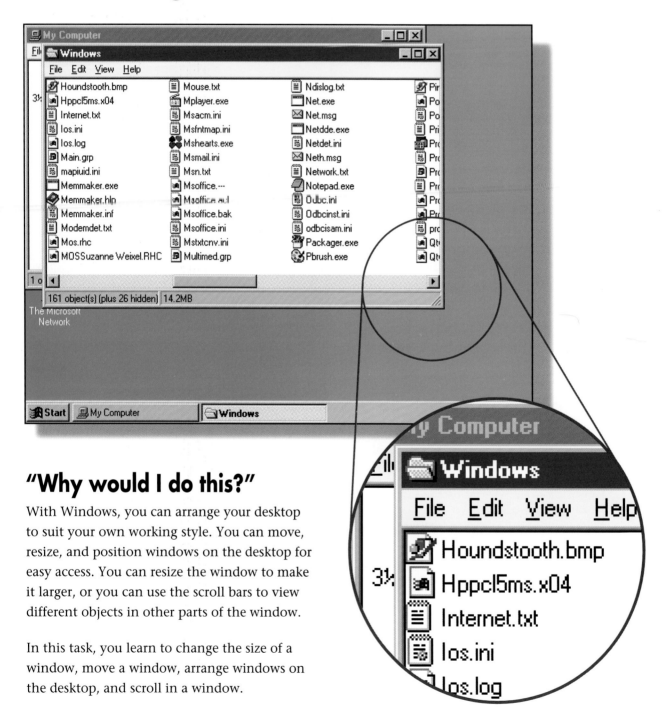

"Why would I do this?"

With Windows, you can arrange your desktop to suit your own working style. You can move, resize, and position windows on the desktop for easy access. You can resize the window to make it larger, or you can use the scroll bars to view different objects in other parts of the window.

In this task, you learn to change the size of a window, move a window, arrange windows on the desktop, and scroll in a window.

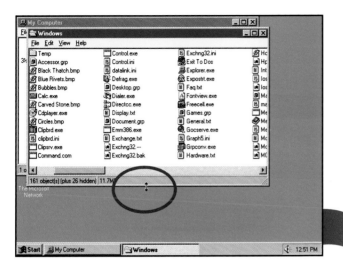

1 Make sure the My Computer and Windows window are open on your desktop (see Task 2). Point at the bottom border of the Windows window. Move the mouse pointer so that it touches the bottom border of the window. When you position it correctly, the mouse pointer changes shape to a double-headed arrow. To resize a window, you drag its borders.

2 Press and hold the left mouse button and move the mouse pointer down toward the bottom of the desktop, dragging the window's border with it. When the window is the size you want, release the mouse button. This step resizes the window.

To quickly change both the height and width of a window, drag one of its corners.

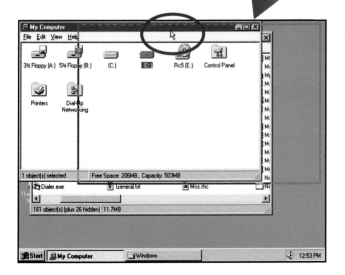

3 Point at the title bar of the My Computer window, press and hold the left mouse button, and move the mouse pointer up and to the right, dragging the window with it. To move a window, you drag the title bar. When the window is in the correct location, release the mouse button. This step moves the window.

4 Move the mouse pointer so that it touches an empty area of the Taskbar, and click the right mouse button. The Taskbar shortcut menu opens. In Windows 95, clicking the right mouse button opens a shortcut menu for the object you are pointing at.

WHY WORRY?

If buttons fill the Taskbar and you have trouble finding an empty area, point at the clock on the right end of the Taskbar, or at one of the thin spaces between the buttons on the Taskbar.

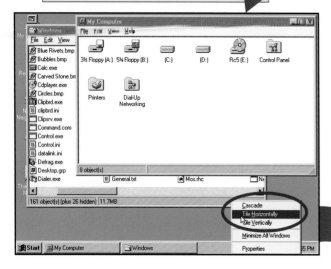

5 Click on **Tile Horizontally** on the Taskbar shortcut menu. When Windows "tiles" open windows, it arranges them so that none of them overlap. When you select Tile **H**orizontally, Windows arranges the windows top to bottom. When you select Tile **V**ertically, Windows arranges the windows side by side. This step arranges the My Computer window and the Windows window top to bottom on the desktop.

6 Right-click on an empty area of the Taskbar. This opens the shortcut menu again. Click on **Cascade**. Cascade is the command that tells Windows to arrange the open windows so that they overlap evenly, leaving a piece of each window visible. This step arranges the My Computer window and the Windows window so that they overlap evenly on the desktop. The Windows window, the last active window, should be on top.

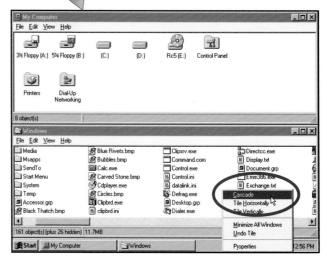

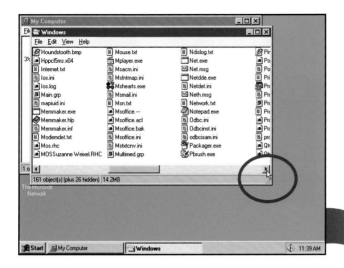

7 Move the mouse pointer so that it touches the arrow at the right end of the horizontal scroll bar. Click on that arrow two times. This shifts the contents of the window so you see additional items. Scroll bars appear along the right side and bottom of a window when there are too many objects in the window to display at once.

NOTE ▼

To quickly switch from one open window to another, click inside the window you want to make active.

8 Click the **Close** button in the Windows window. Clicking the Close button closes the window. The My Computer window is still open on the desktop. ■

WHY WORRY?

If you try to move a window and you change its size instead, you are dragging a border, not the title bar. To move a window you must drag the title bar. Try again.

Minimizing, Maximizing, and Restoring Windows

"Why would I do this?"

If you want to see as much of a window as possible, you can *maximize* it, which means it fills the whole desktop. If you want to keep a window open and available for quick access even though you are not working with it right now, you can *minimize* it, so that it becomes a Taskbar button. In either case, you can restore the window to its previous appearance with a simple click of the mouse.

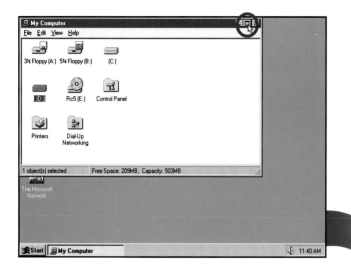

1 Make sure the My Computer window is open on your desktop. Click on the My Computer window's **Maximize** button. The Maximize button is the middle of the three buttons on the right end of the window's title bar. This step maximizes the My Computer window to fill the entire desktop. After you maximize the window, its Maximize button changes to a Restore button.

2 Click on the My Computer window's **Restore** button. This step restores the My Computer window to its previous size and position on the desktop. The Restore button then changes back to a Maximize button.

> **NOTE** ▼
>
> Maximize, Minimize, and Restore are also commands on every window's Control menu and shortcut menu. To open a window's Control menu, click on the window's Control icon (the one to the left of the window's name).

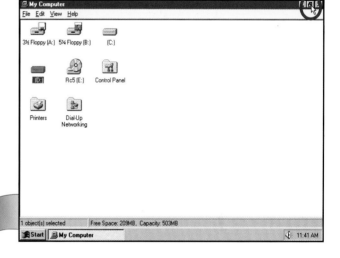

3 Click on the **Minimize** button on the My Computer window's title bar. The Minimize button is the first of the three buttons on the right end of the window's title and has a flat line along its bottom. This step minimizes the My Computer window to a button on the Taskbar.

4 Click the **My Computer** button on the Taskbar. This restores the My Computer window to its previous size and position on the desktop.

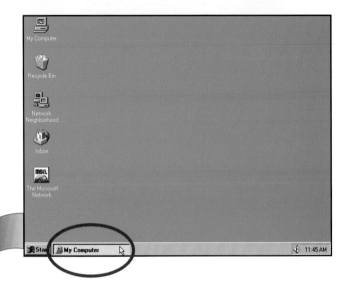

5 Click the **Close** button on the My Computer window's title bar. This closes the My Computer window. ■

NOTE ▼

Minimizing a window is not the same as closing it. A minimized window is still available for use; it is just out of the way. If you minimize a window that has an application program running in it, the application program remains open. When you close a window, the application closes as well. This is why a minimized window still appears on the Taskbar, but a closed window does not.

Getting Help Using Windows 95

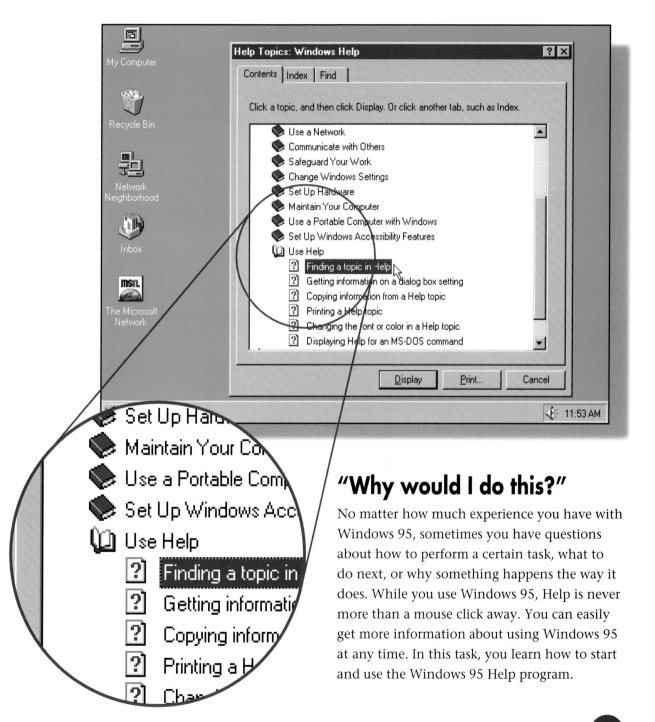

"Why would I do this?"

No matter how much experience you have with Windows 95, sometimes you have questions about how to perform a certain task, what to do next, or why something happens the way it does. While you use Windows 95, Help is never more than a mouse click away. You can easily get more information about using Windows 95 at any time. In this task, you learn how to start and use the Windows 95 Help program.

1 Click the **Start** button on the Taskbar. This step opens the Start menu. The Help program opens from a command on the Start menu.

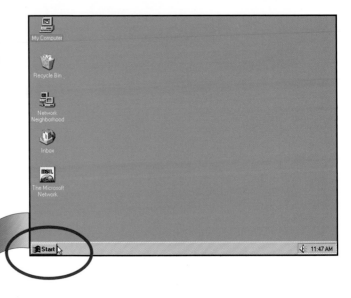

2 Click the word **Help** on the Start menu. Help is the command that starts the Help program. The Help Topics window of the Help program opens on the desktop. You use the Help Topics window to locate the item for which you need more information.

3 Click the **Contents** tab at the top of the Help Topics window to display the table of contents for the Help program. (There are three pages in the Help Topics window: Contents, Index, and Find. In Windows 95, you change pages in a window or dialog box by clicking the appropriate tab.) Then, double-click the topic **How To...**. This step displays all of the subtopics in the How To... section of the Help program.

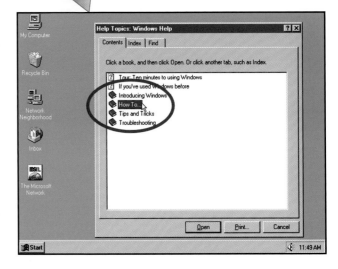

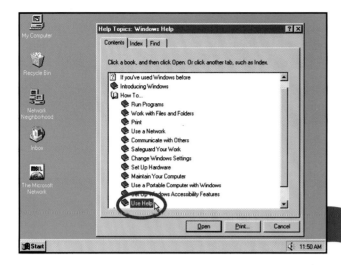

4 Double-click the topic **Use Help**. This step displays additional topics in the How To Use Help section of the Help program. You can tell by the icons that there are no additional subtopics in this section.

NOTE ▼

If the icon next to the Help topic is a book, there are additional help topics. If it is a piece of paper with a question mark, that is the only topic.

5 Double-click the topic **Finding a topic in Help**. This step selects the topic and opens a Windows Help window that provides more information.

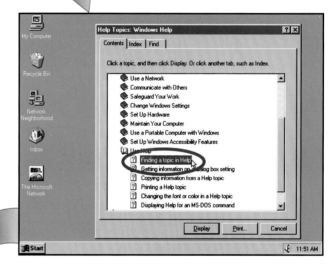

6 Click the **Close** button in the Windows Help window. This step closes the Windows Help program. If you want to access more Help information easily, you can leave the Windows Help program open on top of the desktop, or minimize it to a Taskbar button. ■

NOTE ▼

In some Windows Help windows, you jump from one topic to another by clicking on highlighted or underlined words.

Creating, Naming, and Deleting Folders

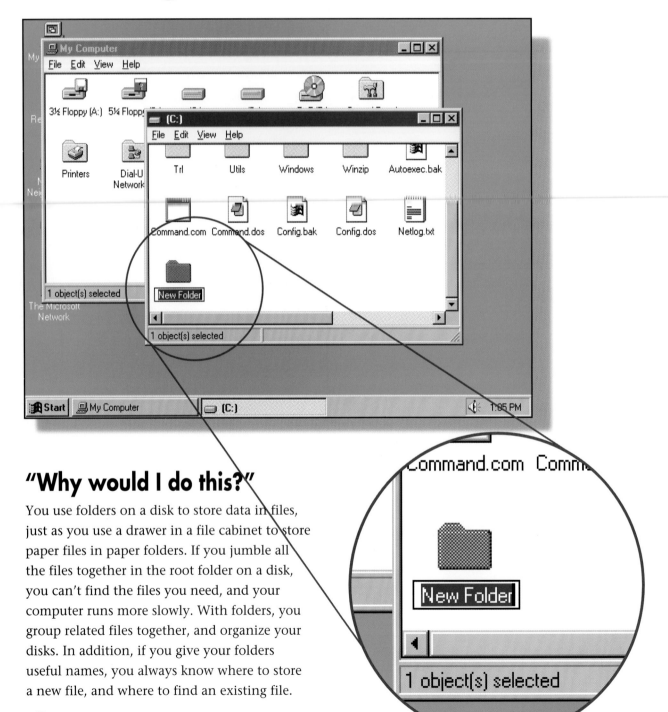

"Why would I do this?"

You use folders on a disk to store data in files, just as you use a drawer in a file cabinet to store paper files in paper folders. If you jumble all the files together in the root folder on a disk, you can't find the files you need, and your computer runs more slowly. With folders, you group related files together, and organize your disks. In addition, if you give your folders useful names, you always know where to store a new file, and where to find an existing file.

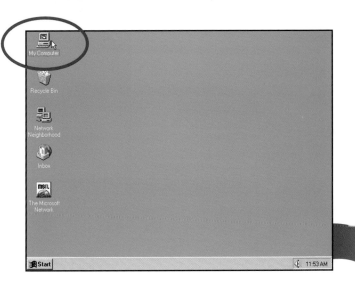

1 Double-click the **My Computer** icon on the Windows 95 desktop. This step opens the My Computer window that contains the icons representing the components of your personal computer system.

2 Double-click the drive **[C:]** icon in the My Computer window. This step opens the drive [C:] window that contains the icons representing the contents of your hard drive [C:]. This is where you want to create the new folder.

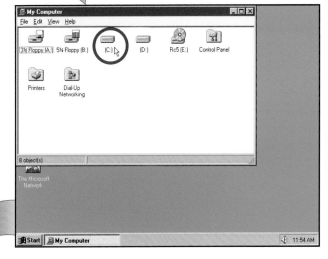

3 Click on the **File** menu item in the drive [C:] window to open the **File** menu.

4 Drag the mouse pointer down to the **New** command. This step displays the nested **New** menu. In Windows 95, you open a nested menu (or submenu) by pointing at the command—you do not have to click the command.

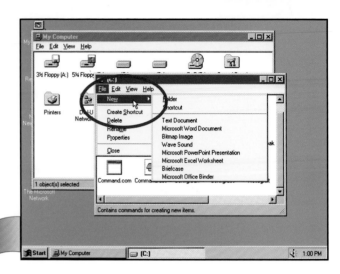

5 Click on **Folder** on the nested **New** menu.

6 Windows creates a new folder—named New Folder—in the active window. The folder name is, by default, in "rename mode," which means you can change the name by typing.

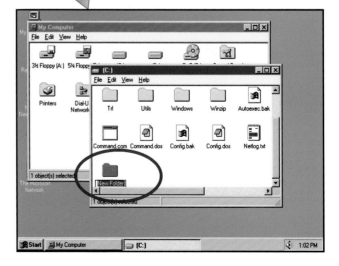

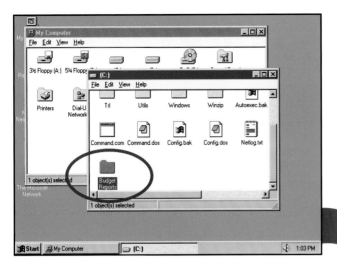

7 Type **Budget Reports** and press **Enter**. This text replaces the default name of the new folder. The new folder—Budget Reports—remains selected. In Windows 95, you can tell when an object is selected because it is highlighted.

WHY WORRY?

If the folder name is not in rename mode, either nothing happens when you type or the computer beeps at you. To change to rename mode, click on the folder name text beneath the folder icon.

8 Press **Del**. This step opens the Confirm Folder Delete dialog box. Before you delete an object, you must confirm the action. Click **Yes** in the Confirm Folder Delete dialog box. Windows 95 deletes the Budget Reports folder from the active window. Windows 95 sends the contents of deleted folders to the Recycle Bin. ■

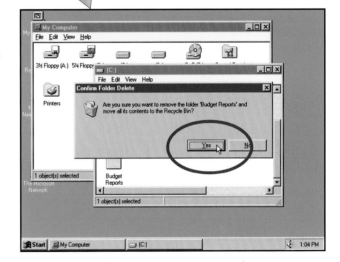

WHY WORRY?

If you delete the wrong object, open the Edit menu in the active window and choose Undo Delete.

NOTE ▼

You can also delete selected objects by choosing Delete from the File menu in the active window, or by dragging the object onto the Recycle Bin icon on the desktop. If you drag the object to the Recycle Bin, Windows 95 does not display the Confirm Delete dialog box.

Formatting Floppy Disks

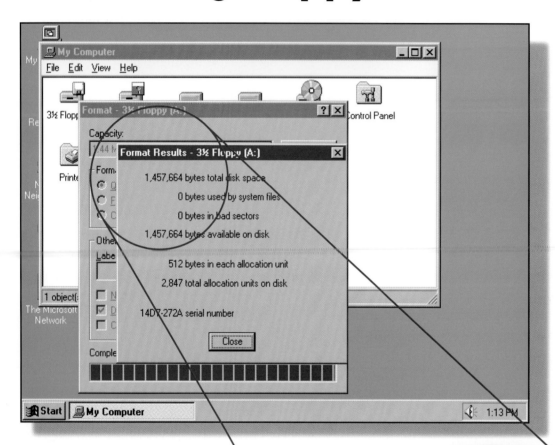

"Why would I do this?"

Before you store data on floppy disks, you must format the disks for use with Windows 95. Formatting creates tracks and sectors on the disk so that Windows 95 can write information and find it again when you need it.

In this task, you format a disk in drive A:.

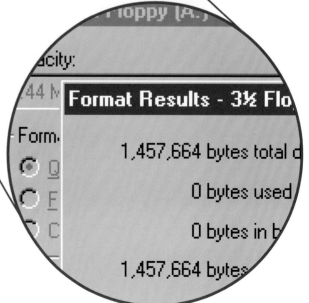

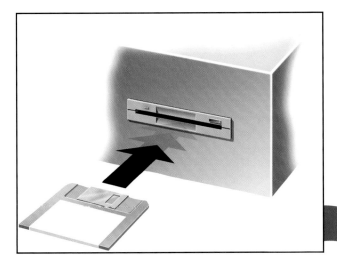

1 Insert a blank floppy disk into drive A:.
This is the disk you are going to format.
Formatting erases all existing data from
the disk, so be sure the disk is blank.

NOTE ▼

You can buy pre-formatted disks, so you
don't have to format the disks before
using them.

2 Double-click the **My Computer** icon on
the desktop. This opens the My Computer
window that contains icons representing
the components of your PC.

3 Click the **Floppy [A:]** icon in the My
Computer window. This step selects drive
A:, making drive A: active.

4 Click on **File** on the My Computer window menu bar to open the **File** menu. Then click the **Format** command.

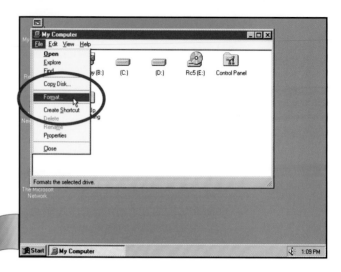

5 The Format dialog box opens. Click the **Start** button in the Format dialog box. This step starts the formatting process.

> **NOTE** ▼
>
> You should never format your hard disk drive. Formatting erases all data from a disk.

6 A status bar at the bottom of the Format dialog box displays the progress of the formatting process. When the format is complete, Windows 95 displays the Format dialog box. Click the **Close** button in the Results dialog box.

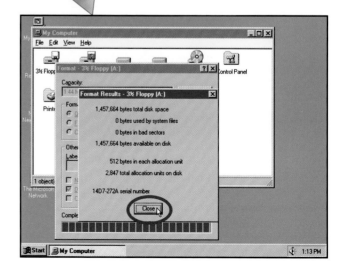

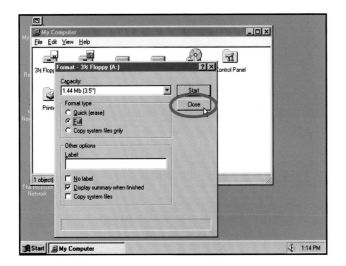

7 Then click the **Close** button in the Format dialog box. ■

WHY WORRY?

Your drive A: may be a different size or capacity than the drive in this task's illustration. Don't worry. The steps to complete the task are the same. To format a disk in a different floppy drive, simply click that drive icon in the My Computer window in step 3 of this task.

NOTE ▼

Use the Quick option in the Format dialog box to quickly reformat a formatted disk or remove data you no longer need from a disk. Use the Full option to format an unformatted disk.

Copying and Renaming Files

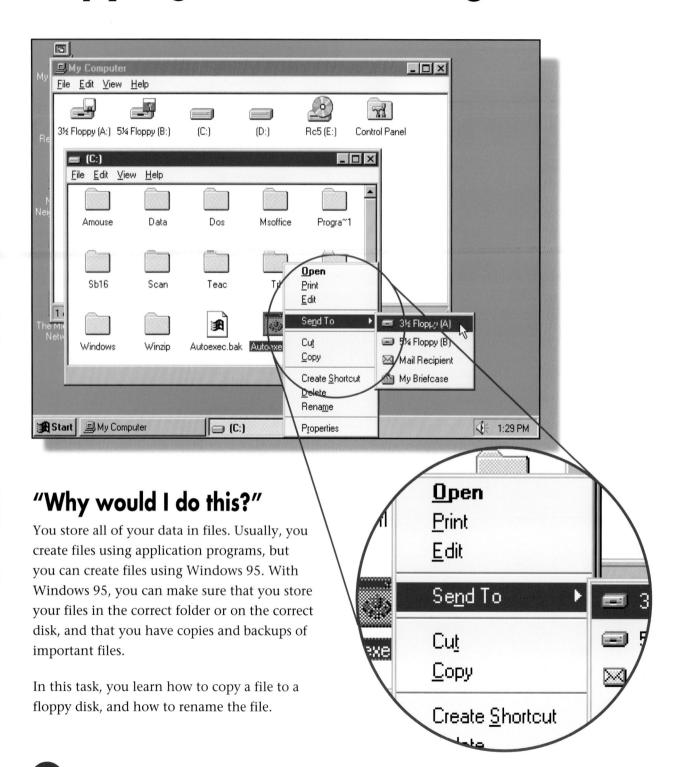

"Why would I do this?"

You store all of your data in files. Usually, you create files using application programs, but you can create files using Windows 95. With Windows 95, you can make sure that you store your files in the correct folder or on the correct disk, and that you have copies and backups of important files.

In this task, you learn how to copy a file to a floppy disk, and how to rename the file.

1 Be sure that you have inserted a formatted floppy disk in Drive A: and opened the My Computer window. Double-click the drive **[C:]** icon in the My Computer window. This step opens the drive [C:] window. Drive [C:] contains the file you are going to copy.

2 Click the icon for the **Autoexec.bat file** in the drive [C:] window. Autoexec.bat is a very important file that your computer needs to start properly. It is a good idea to keep a backup copy of this file on a floppy disk so that if something happens to the original file, you can simply copy the backup to your hard disk.

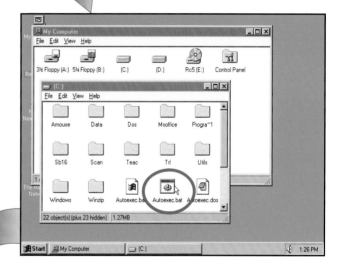

3 Right-click on the Autoexec.bat file icon to open the shortcut menu.

WHY WORRY?

If you do not see the Autoexec.bat file in the drive [C:] window, use the scroll bars to scroll through the window until it appears. Also, if you have file extensions hidden, the file name appears as Autoexec.

4 Point at the **Send To** command on the shortcut menu to open the nested menu.

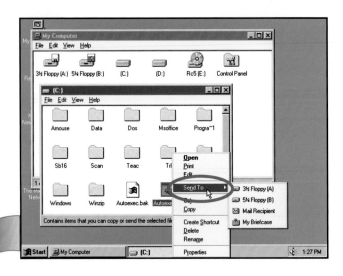

5 Click on **3½ Floppy [A:]** on the nested Send To menu. This step copies the selected file—Autoexec.bat—to the disk in Floppy [A:]. You see a graphic depiction of the file as Windows copies it.

6 Double-click the **3½ Floppy [A:]** icon in the My Computer window. This step opens the Floppy [A:] window. You see the Autoexec.bat file icon in the window.

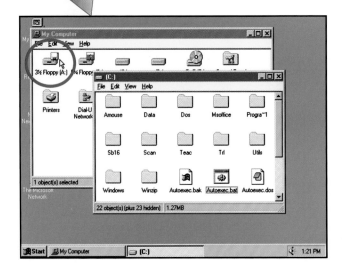

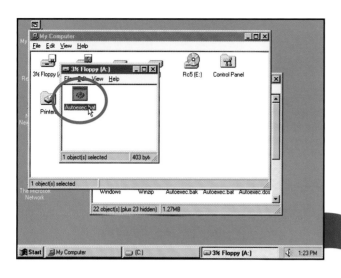

7 Click the **Autoexec.bat file** icon to select it. The icon appears highlighted.

8 Click the file name beneath the selected file icon. This step changes Windows to rename mode, so you can edit the name of the selected file.

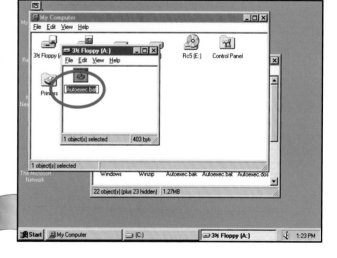

NOTE ▼

To copy more than one file at a time, select the first file, press and hold the Ctrl key on your keyboard, and select the other files. To move a file (or files), simply drag it from its original location to the window representing another disk or another folder.

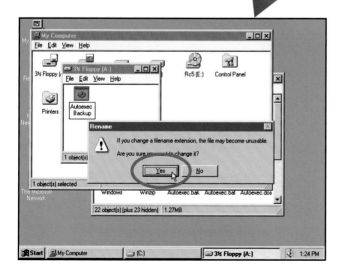

9 Type **Autoexec Backup** and press **Enter**. This replaces the text of the old file name, and opens a dialog box asking you to confirm the action. Click **Yes** in the dialog box. Windows 95 accepts the new file name. ■

Recycling and Restoring Files

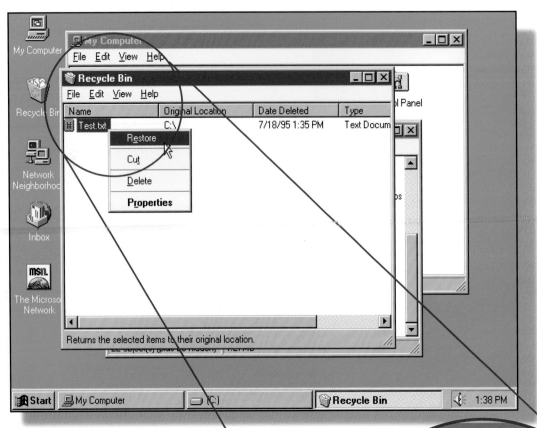

"Why would I do this?"

No matter how much data your disks can hold, someday they will become too full. You won't have enough free space to store more data or to install programs. To make more disk space available, you should delete files that you no longer need. To protect you from accidental deletions, Windows 95 stores deleted files in the Recycle Bin until you empty the bin or restore the files. In this task, you create a new text file and learn how to delete and restore the file using the Recycle Bin.

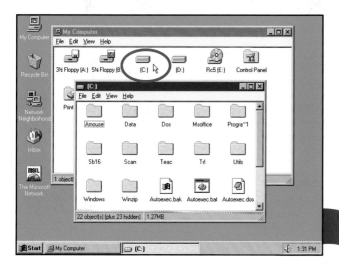

1 Double-click the **My Computer** icon on the desktop to open the My Computer window, then double-click the drive [C:] icon to open the drive [C:] window. As with all Windows 95 tasks, before you perform an action, you must make the correct window active.

2 Click on **File** on the drive [C:] window menu bar to open the **File** menu. Point at **New** to open the **New** nested menu. This is the same menu you use to create a new folder. In this task, you use it to create a text file.

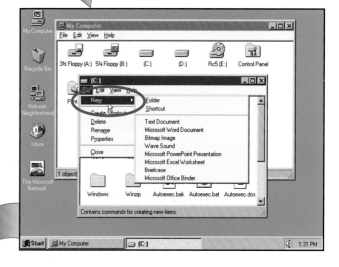

3 Click on **Text Document** on the **New** nested menu. This step creates a new text document on drive [C:].

4 Type **Test** and press **Enter**. This text replaces New Text as the name of the new text document.

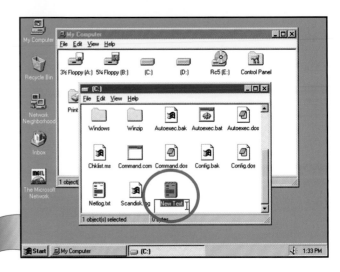

5 Press **Del**. This is the command to delete the selected object—in this case, the Test document. Windows 95 opens the Confirm File Delete dialog box. Click **Yes** in the Confirm File Delete dialog box. Windows 95 sends the document file to the Recycle Bin.

WHY WORRY?

If you cannot see the Recycle Bin icon on the desktop, move, close, or minimize all open windows.

6 Double-click the **Recycle Bin** icon on the desktop. This opens the Recycle Bin window. You see the names of all deleted files listed in the window.

NOTE ▼

The names of deleted files appear in the Recycle Bin window, but the names of deleted folders do not. However, if you restore a file that was in a deleted folder, Windows 95 first restores the folder, then restores the file into it.

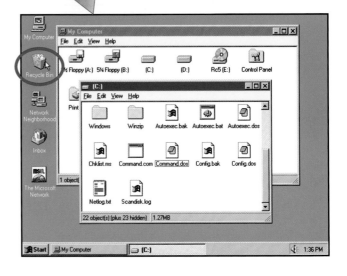

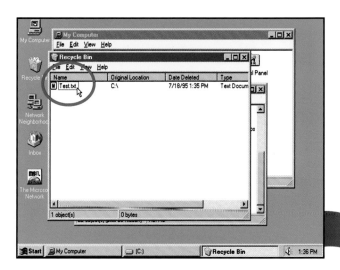

7 Click on **Test.txt** in the Recycle Bin window. This selects the file you want to restore. To select more than one file, press and hold **Ctrl**, and click all of the file names you want to restore.

8 Point at the selected file name, click the right mouse button to open a shortcut menu, and click on **Restore**. This step tells Windows 95 to return the file to its original location—in this case, the drive [C:] window. In Windows 95, you open shortcut menus for most tasks by clicking the right mouse button. ■

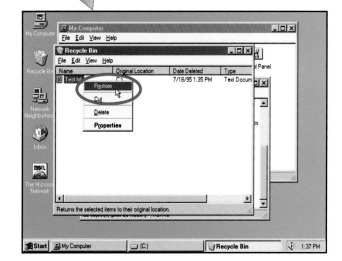

NOTE ▼

To permanently delete all of the files in the Recycle Bin, choose Empty Recycle Bin from the Recycle Bin window's File menu, and choose Yes in the Confirm File Delete dialog box.

Copying Floppy Disks

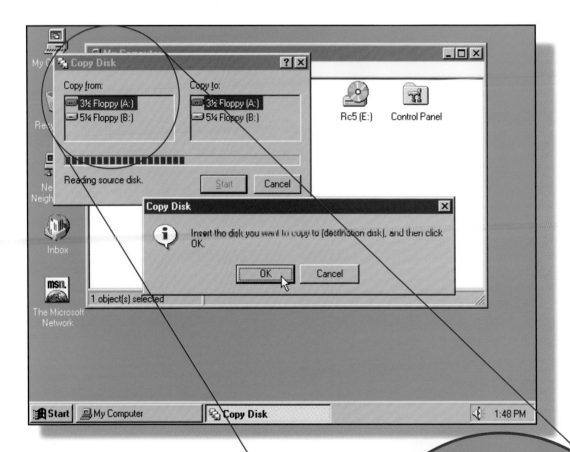

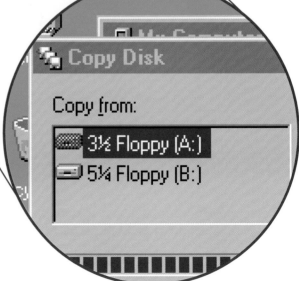

"Why would I do this?"

There are times when you want to copy the entire contents of a disk to another disk of the same size and capacity. For example, if you purchase an application program on floppy disks, you should always make copies of the original disks to use for installation. That way, you don't risk damaging the original disks. Instead of copying the contents of a disk one file at a time, you simply make a duplicate copy of the entire disk.

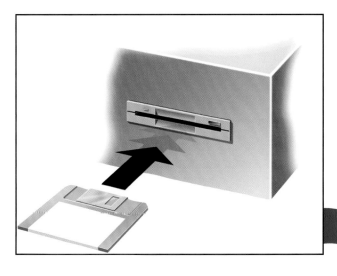

1 Insert the disk you want to copy into drive A:. This is the source disk.

2 Double-click the **My Computer** icon on the Windows 95 desktop to open the My Computer window.

3 Click the **3½ Floppy [A:]** icon in the My Computer window to select drive A.

4 Point at the selected icon, click the right mouse button to open the shortcut menu, and click **Copy Disk**. This step opens the Copy Disk dialog box. You select the source and destination disks in this dialog box.

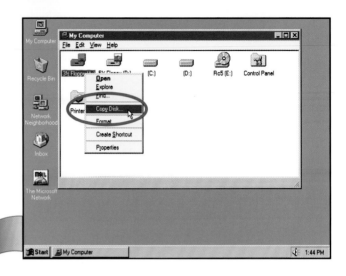

NOTE ▼

If there is data on the destination disk, Windows 95 erases it during the copy procedure. Either use a blank disk, or make sure that you do not need the data on the disk you use.

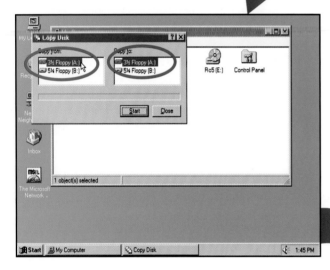

5 Click **3½ Floppy [A:]** in both the **Copy from** and **Copy to** lists. You can only copy a disk to another disk that is the same size and type. If you have two identical disk drives, you use both drives. If you have one disk drive, or two different-sized drives, you must choose the same drive as both the source and destination. This step selects drive A: as both the source and destination drive.

6 Click **Start** in the Copy Disk dialog box. A status bar indicates the progress of the copy procedure. Windows 95 displays another dialog box when it is time to insert the destination disk into drive A.

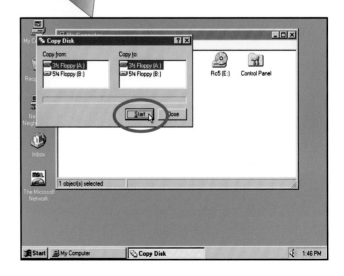

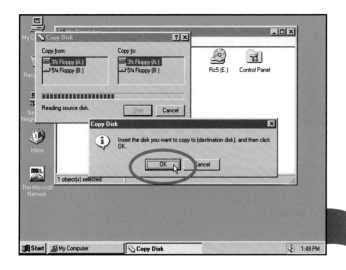

7 Remove the source disk, insert a blank disk into drive A:, and click the **OK** button. This is the destination disk. Windows 95 copies the information from the source disk onto the destination disk. When the copy is complete, the message Copy completed successfully appears in the Copy Disk dialog box.

8 Click **Close** in the Copy Disk dialog box. This step closes the dialog box. ■

WHY WORRY?

If you insert an unformatted disk as the destination disk, Windows 95 formats the disk during the copy procedure.

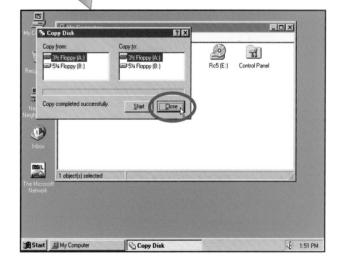

Running Windows Applications

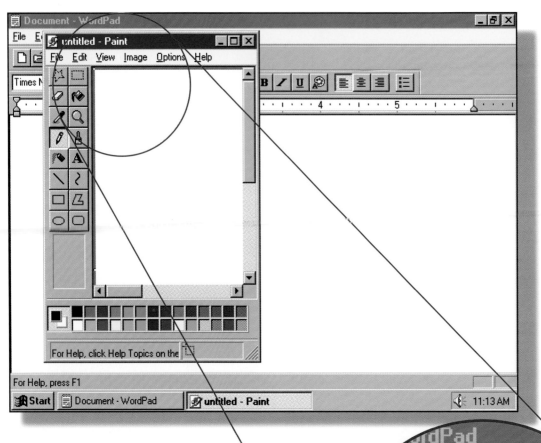

"Why would I do this?"

You use Windows to manage your applications and files, but you use the applications to get your work done. With Windows, you can run more than one application at a time, each in its own window. You need to close all applications before quitting Windows. If you leave any applications open, you run the risk of damaging your files. In this task you learn to start Windows 95 application programs, switch from one program to another, and close the programs.

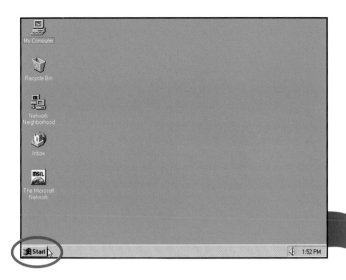

1 Click the **Start** button on the Windows 95 Taskbar. This step opens the Start menu. You use the Start menu to access programs and other features of Windows 95 you frequently use.

2 Point at **Programs** on the Start menu to open the nested Programs menu. The nested Programs menu lists the programs and groups of programs that are installed on your computer.

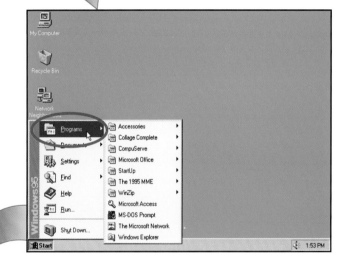

3 Point at **Accessories** on the Programs nested menu to open the nested Accessories menu. This menu lists the programs and groups of programs in the Accessories group.

4 Click on **WordPad** on the Accessories nested menu. This starts WordPad, a word processing application that comes with Windows 95. The WordPad application window opens on the desktop, and Windows 95 adds a button for the untitled WordPad document to the Taskbar.

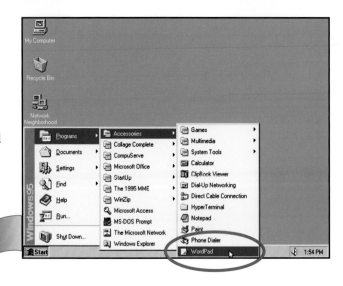

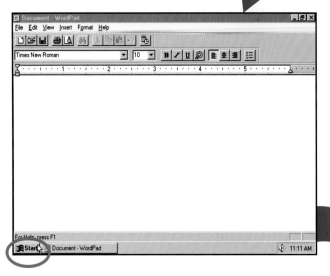

5 You can start more than one application at a time with Windows 95. To open a second application, click the **Start** button on the Taskbar and use the pointer to open the Programs and Accessories nested menus.

6 Click **Paint** on the Accessories nested menu. This step starts the Paint accessory, a drawing application that comes with Windows 95. The Paint window opens on the desktop, and Windows 95 adds a button for the untitled Paint document to the Taskbar.

NOTE ▼

You can open as many windows as you want, until you run out of memory. Keep in mind, however, that the more windows you open, the slower your system runs.

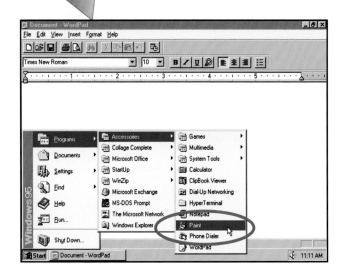

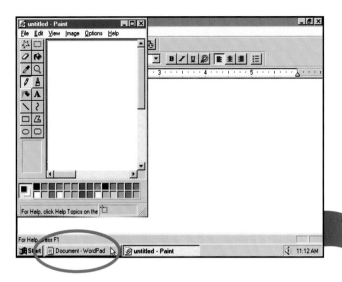

7 Click the **WordPad** button on the Taskbar, making the WordPad application window active rather than the Paint application window.

NOTE ▼

With a keyboard, you can switch from one open application to another. Press and hold Alt, and press Tab. Each time you press Tab, you select the icon for another open application. When you select the application you want to make active, release the keys.

8 Click on the **Close** button on the right end of the WordPad title bar. This step quits the WordPad application and closes the WordPad application window. Paint is still running.

WHY WORRY?

You should always save the files you work with before quitting an application. If you forget to save and try to quit, the application displays a dialog box asking if you want to save the changes. Choose Yes to save the changes, or choose No to quit without saving the changes.

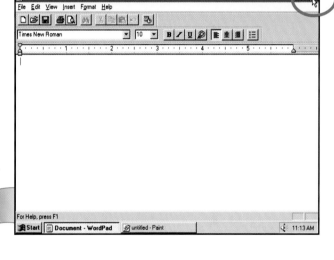

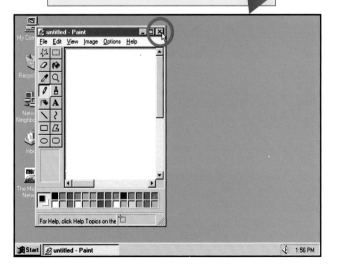

9 Click on the **Close** button on the right end of the Paint title bar. This step quits the Paint application and closes the Paint application window. ■

NOTE ▼

If you cannot see the complete name of a button on the Taskbar, point at the button with the mouse pointer. A little note, called a ToolTip, appears above the button telling you the name of the application.

Creating a Program Shortcut

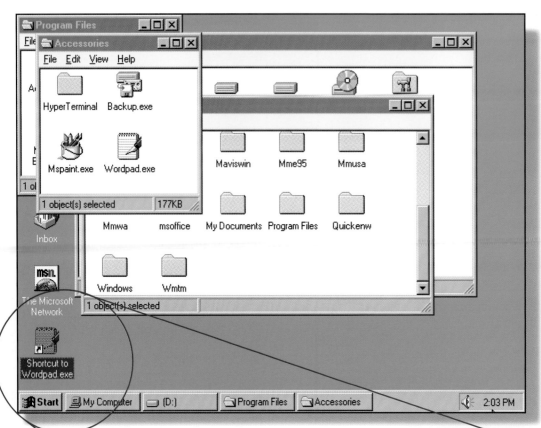

"Why would I do this?"

The Start menu provides an easy way to start programs in Windows 95, but sometimes you have to wade through several layers of nested menus. If you use a program frequently, you can create a program shortcut icon on the desktop. Then, to start the program, you simply double-click the icon on the desktop.

In this task, you learn how to create a shortcut on the desktop.

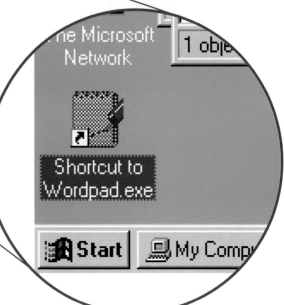

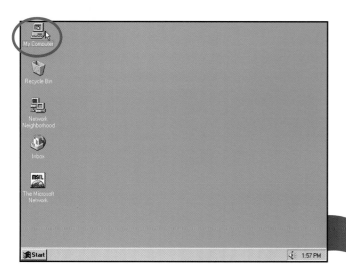

1 Double-click the **My Computer** icon on the desktop to open the My Computer window.

2 Double-click the drive **[C:]** icon in the My Computer window to open the drive [C:] window.

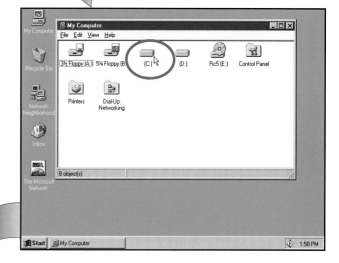

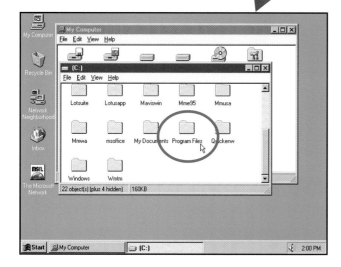

3 Double-click the **Program Files folder** in the drive [C:] window to open the Program Files window. You may have to scroll through the drive C: window to find the Program Files folder.

4 Double-click the **Accessories folder** in the Program Files window to open the Accessories window.

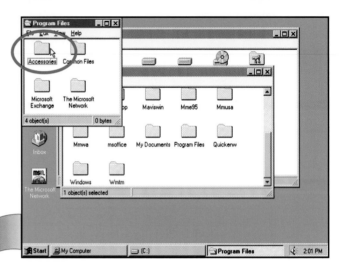

5 Point at the **Wordpad.exe file** icon, press and hold the left mouse button, and drag the mouse pointer so that it points at a blank area of the desktop.

6 To create a shortcut, you drag the program file onto the desktop.

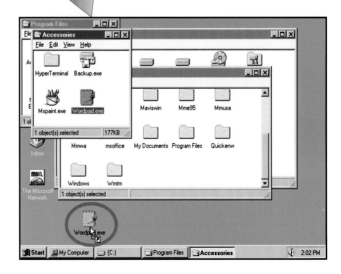

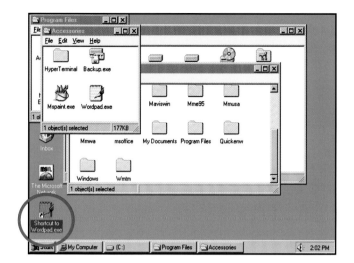

7 Release the left mouse button. This step creates a shortcut to the WordPad application program. From now on, to start WordPad, simply double-click the **Shortcut to Wordpad.exe** icon. ■

WHY WORRY?

If you release the left mouse button too soon, Windows 95 does not create the shortcut. Just try again.

NOTE ▼

You can rename the shortcut icon on the desktop. Click the icon to select it, and click the icon name to change to rename mode. Type the new name and press Enter. To delete a shortcut icon, click the icon to select it. Then press Del. If Windows prompts you to confirm the deletion, click Yes. Deleting a shortcut icon does not delete the program files from your hard disk.

This part of the book provides information about how to use common DOS commands. Although most people use Windows 3.1 or Windows 95 to manage their computers, there may be times when you find yourself face to face with the DOS prompt. For example, you may accidentally close Windows 3.1 and display the DOS prompt, or you may have to use a computer that does not have Windows installed. If that happens, it is important that you feel comfortable with DOS and that you know how to use DOS to perform certain basic directory and file management tasks.

When working in DOS, you must keep in mind how information is stored on your hard disk. Related files are kept within their own directories (or folders) on the disk. Within these directories, groups of files are put into subdirectories. A typical hard disk has many levels of subdirectories within its directories.

In order to complete the tasks in this section, you need a computer that has DOS installed on your hard disk or on a floppy diskette that fits in your A: drive. If your computer is running Windows 3.1 or Windows 95, you must access the DOS prompt. If you have Windows 3.1, double-click on the **MS-DOS** icon in the Main program group. In Windows 95, click on the **Start** menu, click on **Programs**, and click on **MS-DOS Prompt**. In both Windows 3.1 and Windows 95, you see a window with the DOS prompt. Enter any commands as normal and press **Enter**. To return to Windows 3.1 or Windows 95, type Exit at the DOS prompt and press **Enter**.

DOS is very particular about the way you type in commands. You must use the correct command name and you must type the command precisely using the correct *syntax* (the form or order in which you type commands), or DOS will not execute the command. Keep these rules in mind:

- Start typing the command in the first space to the right of the DOS prompt. If you press the space bar before typing the command, DOS will not recognize the command.

- You can type a command in uppercase or lowercase letters. This is probably the only thing DOS isn't particular about.

- DOS doesn't execute the command until you press **Enter**.

- You can correct mistakes on the command line before you press **Enter**. Press **Backspace** to delete the command, and type it again, or press **Esc** to start a new command line.

- If you press **Enter** and realize you made a mistake, you may be able to cancel the command by pressing **Esc**, **Ctrl+C**, or **Ctrl+Break**.

- Some commands use *switches* to change the way DOS displays the command's output. A switch is a slash character (/) usually followed by a letter that you type in after a DOS command. For example, you use the /P switch with some commands to display only one screen of information at a time. When you type a switch, do not leave a space between the slash and the letter.

- Some commands use parameters to control the way DOS executes the command. A parameter is often the name of the file or directory you want the command to affect. When you type a parameter, leave a space between the command name and the parameter name.

- When you type a file name, remember to type a backslash character (\) to separate directories from other directories and the file name.

- DOS executes some commands only if \DOS is the current directory. If you see the message `Bad command or filename` when you try to enter a command, you may need to change to the \DOS directory by typing **CD\DOS.**

Some Common DOS Commands

Command	Result	EXAMPLE
DIR	List files in a directory	DIR C:
COPY	Copy files from one location to another	COPY MEMO.DOC A:
CD	Change the current directory	CD\DOS
MD	Make a directory	MD \DATA
DEL	Delete a file	DEL *.DOC
UNDELETE	Undelete a file	UNDELETE *.DOC
RENAME	Rename a file	RENAME MEMO.DOC LETTER.DOC
FORMAT	Format a disk	FORMAT A:
MOVE	Move files from one location to another	MOVE MEMO.DOC A:
DISKCOPY	Make an exact duplicate of a floppy disk	DISKCOPY A: A:
CLS	Clear the screen of everything but the DOS prompt	CLS
MEM	Display a report of system memory usage	MEM
TIME	Display the current time and enter a new time	TIME 1:58p
DATE	Display the current date and enter a new date	DATE 08-08-95

Changing Disks and Directories

"Why would I do this?"

DOS executes most commands on the current drive in the current directory (or folder). Although you can add parameters to the command to specify a different file or directory, it's usually easier to make the different drive or directory current. Then you just type the command without additional parameters.

In this task, you learn how to change to a different disk and to the root directory. Before you begin this task, insert a formatted disk into drive A.

1 At the DOS prompt, type **A:** and press **Enter**. A: is the name of the drive you want to make current. DOS switches to drive A and displays the name of the current drive (now A) in the DOS prompt (usually as A:\>). To change drives, you type the name of the drive and press **Enter**.

> **NOTE** ▼
>
> The name of a disk drive is a letter followed by a colon (:), so A: is the name of floppy disk drive A, and C: is the name of hard drive C.

2 At the DOS prompt, type **C:** and press **Enter** to change back to drive C.

> **WHY WORRY?**
>
> If you see the message, Not ready reading drive A Abort, Retry, Fail? it means that there is no disk in the drive, or that you inserted the disk incorrectly. Put a formatted disk in the drive, and press R to try again.
>
> If you see the message General failure reading drive A Abort, Retry, Fail?, it means that the disk you inserted in the drive is not formatted. Insert a formatted disk, and press R to try again.

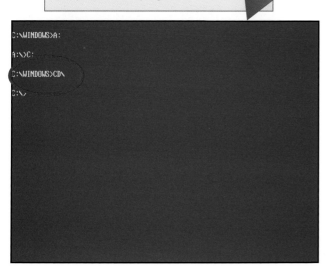

3 At the DOS prompt, type **CD** and press **Enter**. CD is the command that tells DOS to change directories, and \ is the symbol for the root directory. DOS changes to the root directory. DOS displays the name of the current directory (in this case, the root) in the DOS prompt. To change to a directory, use the CD command followed by the directory name. From there, you can progress to subdirectories within the current directory by typing **CD** and the subdirectory name ■

Displaying Directory Lists

```
C:\>DIR

 Volume in drive C has no label
 Volume Serial Number is 1E28-5CE4
 Directory of C:\

AUTOEXEC BAT          403   06-21-95  4:50p
DOS          <DIR>          01-08-95 11:28a
WINDOWS      <DIR>          01-08-95 11:59a
AMOUSE       <DIR>          01-08-95 11:55a
TEAC         <DIR>          04-21-95 10:36a
UTILS        <DIR>          01-08-95  3:42p
WINZIP       <DIR>          01-27-95  5:49p
MSOFFICE     <DIR>          03-12-95 11:56a
SB16         <DIR>          04-22-95  7:51p
SCAN         <DIR>          04-22-95  7:53p
TRL          <DIR>          04-21-95 12:22p
TEMP         <DIR>          07-06-95  1:18p
CONFIG   SYS        1,051   06-28-95  2:55p
COMMAND  COM       92,870   06-09-95  4:00a
DATA         <DIR>          04-22-95  7:34p
         3 file(s)         94,324 bytes
        12 dir(s)       1,163,264 bytes free

C:\>
```

"Why would I do this?"

Displaying directory lists enables you to see the contents of a disk or directory, which is useful for finding files and for verifying the location of files. You should always display a directory list before formatting a disk, creating a directory, copying or moving files, or deleting files and directories. That way, you avoid mistakes, such as erasing or overwriting important information.

```
C:\>DIR

Volume in drive C has no label
Volume Serial Number is 1E28-5CE4
Directory of C:\

AUTOEXEC BAT           403  06-21-95   4:50p
DOS           <DIR>         01-08-95  11:28a
WINDOWS       <DIR>         01-08-95  11:59a
AMOUSE        <DIR>         01-08-95  11:55a
TEAC          <DIR>         04-21-95  10:36a
UTILS         <DIR>         01-08-95   3:42p
WINZIP        <DIR>         01-27-95   5:49p
MSOFFICE      <DIR>         03-12-95  11:56a
SB16          <DIR>         04-22-95   7:51p
SCAN          <DIR>         04-22-95   7:53p
TRL           <DIR>         04-21-95  12:22p
TEMP          <DIR>         07-06-95   1:18p
CONFIG   SYS         1,051  06-28-95   2:55p
COMMAND  COM        92,870  06-09-95   4:00a
DATA          <DIR>         01 22-95   7:34p
        3 file(s)        94,324 bytes
       12 dir(s)      1,163,264 bytes free

C:\>
```

1 At the DOS prompt in the root directory, type **DIR** and press **Enter**. DIR is the command that tells DOS to display a list of all files in the directory in which DOS is currently working. In this case, the current directory is the root (\). Pressing Enter tells DOS to execute the command. You see on-screen a list of the files and directories the current directory contains. DOS displays the DOS prompt at the bottom of the list when it is done listing the files.

2 At the DOS prompt at the bottom of the screen, type **DIR**, press the **space bar** once, and type **\DOS**. \DOS is the path to the DOS directory, a subdirectory of the root. If you follow the DIR command with a parameter specifying a different directory or drive, DOS displays the contents of the specified directory or drive.

> **NOTE** ▼
>
> If the directory is on a different disk, type the disk name at the beginning of the path, like this A:\DOS.

```
C:\>DIR

Volume in drive C has no label
Volume Serial Number is 1E28-5CE4
Directory of C:\

AUTOEXEC BAT           403  06-21-95   4:50p
DOS           <DIR>         01-08-95  11:28a
WINDOWS       <DIR>         01-08-95  11:59a
AMOUSE        <DIR>         01-08-95  11:55a
TEAC          <DIR>         04-21-95  10:36a
UTILS         <DIR>         01-08-95   3:42p
WINZIP        <DIR>         01-27-95   5:49p
MSOFFICE      <DIR>         03-12-95  11:56a
SB16          <DIR>         04-22-95   7:51p
SCAN          <DIR>         04-22-95   7:53p
TRL           <DIR>         04-21-95  12:22p
TEMP          <DIR>         07-06-95   1:18p
CONFIG   SYS         1,051  06-28-95   2:55p
COMMAND  COM        92,870  06-09-95   4:00a
DATA          <DIR>         04-22-95   7:34p
        3 file(s)        94,324 bytes
       12 dir(s)      1,163,264 bytes free

C:\>DIR \DOS
```

```
MWAVDRVL DLL     7,744  05-31-94   6:22a
MWAVMGR  DLL    21,712  05-31-94   6:22a
MWAVSCAN DLL   151,568  05-31-94   6:22a
MWAVSOS  DLL     7,888  05-31-94   6:22a
MWAVTSR  EXE    17,328  05-31-94   6:22a
VSAFE    COM    62,576  05-31-94   6:22a
MWGRAFIC DLL    36,944  05-31-94   6:22a
CHKLIST  MS      2,349  02-24-95   2:03p
UNDELETE INI        45  02-16-95  12:41p
CC50219A FUL     1,856  02-19-95  12:28p
MWAV     INI       354  02-24-95   2:15p
DEFAULT  SET     4,482  04-17-95   5:10p
DEFAULT  SLT       821  04-17-95   5:10p
DEFAULT  CAT        66  04-17-95   5:10p
DATA1    SET     4,488  02-19-95   1:01p
DATA1    SLT       716  02-19-95   1:01p
CC50329A FUL     2,624  03-29-95   4:46p
CC50417A FUL     8,000  04-17-95   5:01p
QBASIC   EXE   194,309  05-31-94   6:22a
QBASIC   HLP   130,881  05-31-94   6:22a
QBASIC   INI       132  02-26-94  11:56a
       __ file(s)      4,066,710 bytes
        3 dir(s)      1,163,264 bytes free

C:\>
```

3 Press **Enter** to tell DOS to execute the command. You see on-screen a list of the files and directories the \DOS directory contains. DOS displays the DOS prompt at the bottom of the list.

> **WHY WORRY?**
>
> Type DIR /W (for "wide") to display the directory listing in more columns all the way across the screen, or DIR /P (for "page") to display the list one page at a time.

161

4 At the DOS prompt at the bottom of the list, type **DIR**, press the **space bar** once, and type **/S**. /S is the switch that tells DOS to display the contents of the current directory and all subdirectories. If the current directory is the root, DOS displays the contents of every directory on the disk. You can use the /S switch to ask DOS to look through all the directories to find a specific file.

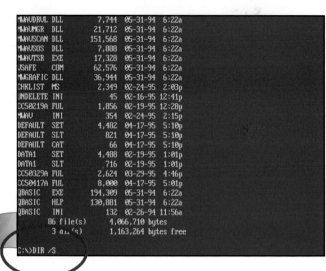

5 Following the /S switch, press the **space bar** once, type **README.TXT**, and press **Enter**. README.TXT is the name of a file stored somewhere on your disk. When you follow the DIR command with a file name, DOS displays information about only the specified file. Because you use the /S switch with a file name, DOS displays information about the README.TXT file.

6 At the DOS prompt, type **CLS** and press **Enter**. CLS is the command that tells DOS to clear all information except the DOS prompt from the screen. ■

> **NOTE** ▼
>
> You can use wild-card characters in the file specification to display a group of files. For example, to see only files with a .DOC extension, type *.DOC.

A Default Directory List Has the Following Information:

Item	What It Tells You
File name	The first part of the file name—up to eight characters long—appears in the first column.
File extension	The file extension—up to three characters long—appears in the second column. Directories do not have file extensions.
<DIR>	To indicate a directory, DOS displays <DIR> in the third column.
File size	The size of a file in bytes appears in the third column. (Directories do not include a size.)
Date	The date you created or last modified the file appears in the next column.
Time	The time you created or last modified the file appears in the last column. The two lines after the listing display the number of files, the total number of bytes used, and the number of bytes remaining unused (free).

Formatting Floppy Disks

```
C:\>FORMAT A:
Insert new diskette for drive A:
and press ENTER when ready...

Checking existing disk format.
Verifying 1.44M
Format complete.

Volume label (11 characters, ENTER for none)? STORAGE

    1,457,664 bytes total disk space
    1,457,664 bytes available on disk

        512 bytes in each allocation unit.
      2,847 allocation units available on disk.

Volume Serial Number is 0A2C-14EF

Format another (Y/N)?N
```

"Why would I do this?"

Before you store data on floppy disks, you must format the disks for use with DOS. Formatting creates tracks and sectors on the disk so DOS can write information there. It also creates a table on the disk where DOS records the location of data (called the *file allocation table*, or *FAT*). When DOS goes to find information on the disk, it consults the FAT to find the correct location. In this task, you learn how to format a floppy disk in drive A and to reformat a formatted disk.

```
C:\>FORMAT A:
Insert new disk
and press ENTER

Checking existi
Verifying 1.44
Format compl
```

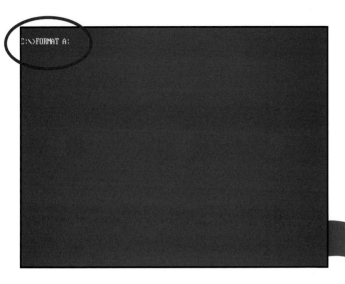

1 At the DOS prompt in the root directory, type **FORMAT**, press the **space bar** once, and type **A:**. FORMAT is the command that tells DOS to format a diskette. A: is the parameter that tells DOS to format the disk in drive A. Never format your hard drive (C:), or you will lose all information stored on it.

NOTE ▼

If you have two diskette drives, you can format disks in either one. To format a disk in drive B, type FORMAT B:.

2 Press **Enter** to tell DOS to execute the command. DOS responds with a prompt telling you to insert a new diskette in the drive.

NOTE ▼

Formatting erases all data that the disk contains, so you should be sure that the disk is blank, or that you do not want the files on it anymore.

3 Insert the floppy disk into the drive and press **Enter**. DOS formats the disk. On-screen, you see information about how the formatting is progressing.

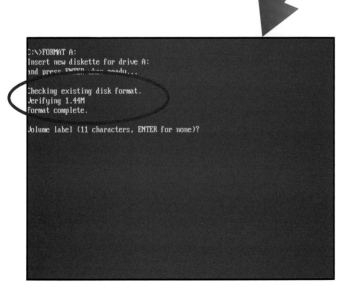

4 When the formatting is complete, DOS asks you to enter an optional *volume label*—a name for the disk. Type **STORAGE**—the volume label for this example—and press **Enter**. DOS displays the amount of storage space available on the disk, and asks if you want to format another disk. Type **N** and press **Enter** to return to the DOS prompt.

```
C:\>FORMAT A:
Insert new diskette for drive A:
and press ENTER when ready...

Checking existing disk format.
Verifying 1.44M
Format complete.

Volume label (11 characters, ENTER for none)? STORAGE

 1,457,664 bytes total disk space
 1,457,664 bytes available on disk

        512 bytes in each allocation unit.
      2,847 allocation units available on disk.

Volume Serial Number is 0A2C-14EF

Format another (Y/N)?N
```

> **NOTE** ▼
>
> If you do not want to enter a volume label, simply press Enter at the Volume label prompt.

```
C:\>FORMAT/Q A:
```

5 At the DOS prompt, type **FORMAT/Q**, press the **space bar** once, and type **A:**, or type **FORMAT A: /Q**. FORMAT is the command that tells DOS to format a diskette, /Q is the switch that tells DOS to perform a quick format, and A: is the parameter that tells DOS to format the disk in drive A. You can use the /Q switch to quickly format a disk that has already been formatted—but remember that this removes any data on the disk.

6 Press **Enter** to execute the command. DOS responds by asking you to insert a disk into the drive. Insert a formatted floppy disk into the drive (for this example, use the disk you just formatted) and press **Enter**. DOS formats the disk. On-screen, you see information about how the formatting is progressing. When the formatting is complete, DOS asks you to enter a volume label.

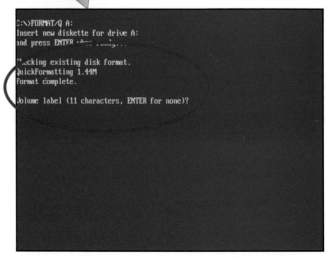

```
C:\>FORMAT/Q A:
Insert new diskette for drive A:
and press ENTER when ready...

Checking existing disk format.
QuickFormatting 1.44M
Format complete.

Volume label (11 characters, ENTER for none)?
```

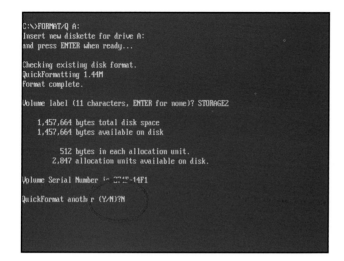

```
C:\>FORMAT/Q A:
Insert new diskette for drive A:
and press ENTER when ready...

Checking existing disk format.
QuickFormatting 1.44M
Format complete.

Volume label (11 characters, ENTER for none)? STORAGE2

    1,457,664 bytes total disk space
    1,457,664 bytes available on disk

        512 bytes in each allocation unit.
      2,847 allocation units available on disk.

Volume Serial Number is 271E-14F1

QuickFormat another (Y/N)?N
```

7 Type **STORAGE2**—the new volume label for this reformatted disk—and press **Enter**. DOS displays the amount of storage space available on the disk and asks if you want to format another disk. Type **N**, and press **Enter** to return to the DOS prompt. ■

NOTE ▼

If you do not want to enter a volume label, just press Enter at the Volume label prompt.

Setting the Clock/Calendar

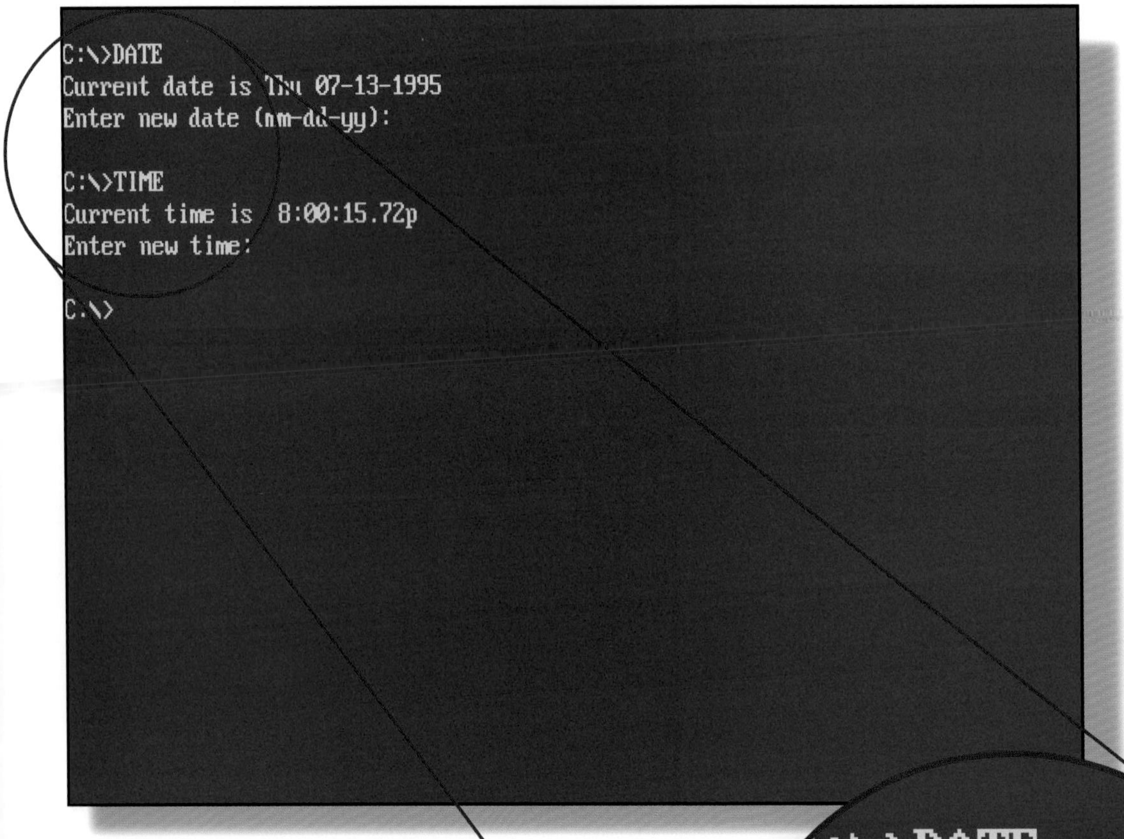

```
C:\>DATE
Current date is Thu 07-13-1995
Enter new date (mm-dd-yy):

C:\>TIME
Current time is  8:00:15.72p
Enter new time:

C:\>
```

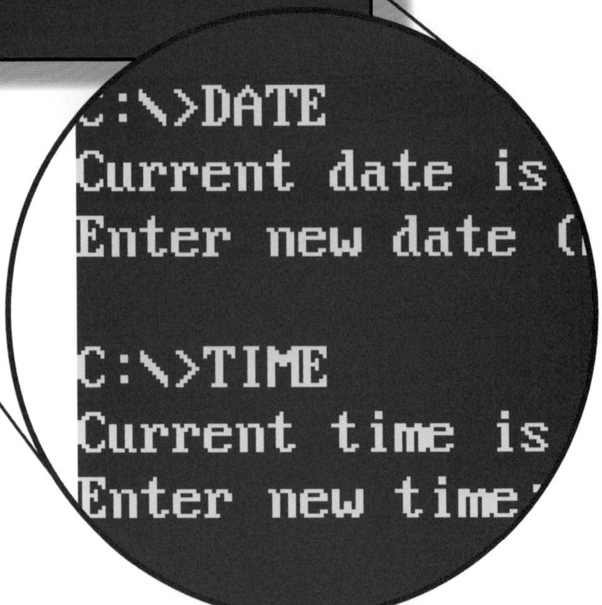

```
C:\>DATE
Current date is
Enter new date (

C:\>TIME
Current time is
Enter new time
```

"Why would I do this?"

DOS keeps track of the date and time using a built-in clock/calendar. It uses the date and time to mark the files that you create with a *timestamp* that shows the date and time you created or last modified a file. The timestamp helps you determine which is the most recent copy of a file and when you last worked on a certain project. You see the timestamp in a standard directory list. In this task, you learn to check and change the current date and time.

1 At the DOS prompt, type **DATE** and press **Enter**. DOS displays the current date, and prompts you to enter a new date. Type a new date using the format mm-dd-yy: the month (01 through 12), a hyphen, the day (01 through 31), another hyphen, and the last two digits of the year (for example, type **07-13-95** for July 13, 1995). Then press **Enter**. DOS changes the date on the built-in clock/calendar.

2 At the DOS prompt, type **TIME** and press **Enter**. DOS displays the current time and prompts you to enter a new time. Type the hour, a colon, and the minutes. Then type either **a**, for a.m., or **p**, for p.m. For example, type **8:08p**. Press **Enter**.

NOTE ▼

You can include the seconds and the tenths of a second in the time if you want to be precise. Simply type a colon after the minutes, type the seconds, type a period, and type the tenths of a second. Then, type a for a.m.

3 To check the date, type **DATE** and press **Enter**. Press **Enter** again to leave the date as is. To check the time, type **TIME** and press **Enter**. Press **Enter** again to leave the time as is. ■

Checking Your System Memory

```
C:\>MEM

Memory Type        Total       Used       Free
                   ------      -----      -----

Conventional        640K        96K       544K
Upper               155K       111K        43K
Reserved            384K       384K         0K
Extended (XMS)    15,205K     3,965K    11,240K
                  --------    -------   --------

Total memory      16,384K     4,557K    11,827K


Total under 1 MB    795K       209K       587K

Largest executable program size     544K  (556,656 bytes)
Largest free upper memory block      43K   (44,272 bytes)
MS-DOS is resident in the high memory area.


C:\>
```

"Why would I do this?"

To run your operating system and your application programs, you need to have enough RAM (or memory) installed on your computer. You can use DOS to find out how much memory is available, so you can determine if you have enough to run new programs.

In this task, you learn how to find out how much, and what type, memory you have.

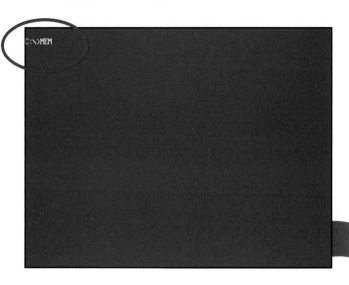

1 At the DOS prompt type **MEM** and press **Enter**. MEM is the command that tells DOS to display a status report about your system memory. You see on-screen a chart that describes the different kinds of memory that you have installed, and the amount of each kind that is available for use.

2 Look for the total amount of free conventional memory and the total amount of free memory of all kinds. DOS runs all programs in conventional memory, but you may be able to make use of upper or extended memory to free more conventional memory.

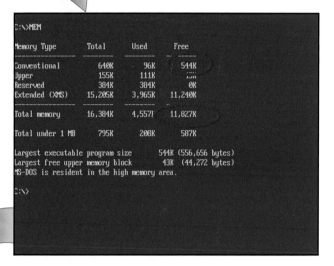

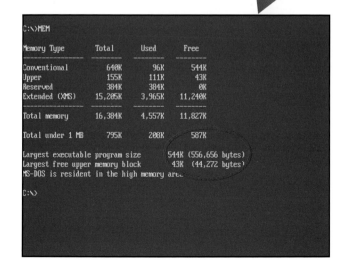

3 Look for the largest executable program size. This tells you how much memory is available to run additional application programs. You use this information to determine whether you need more memory. ■

WHY WORRY?

If you do not have enough free memory, you may be able to use a memory manager, such as DOS's MEMMAKER, to make more conventional memory available.

Running Applications

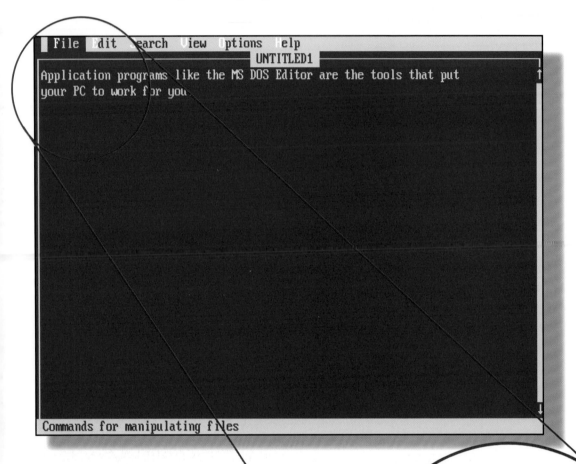

"Why would I do this?"

When you start an application program, DOS loads it into memory so that you can use it. While an application program is running, you see the application's interface on-screen, instead of the DOS prompt. Instead of using DOS commands, you use the commands that control the application. When you finish using the application, you exit from it and return to the DOS prompt. In this task you learn how to start an application program from the DOS prompt, and how to exit back to the DOS prompt.

1 At the DOS prompt, type **CD\DOS** and press **Enter**. CD is the command that tells DOS to change directories, and \DOS is the path to the DOS directory. To start most applications, the current directory must be the directory that contains the program files. In this case, the program files used to run the MS-DOS Editor are in the DOS directory.

2 At the DOS prompt, type **EDIT** and press **Enter**. EDIT is the command that starts the Editor. The MS-DOS Editor appears on-screen. If necessary, press **Esc** to remove the Welcome box from the screen.

> **NOTE** ▼
>
> You start most DOS programs by typing the program name, or an abbreviation of the program name, at the DOS prompt. To find the command to use to start an application, check the application's user manual.

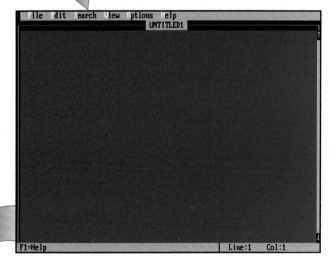

3 Press **Alt** to activate the menu bar. The selection letters become highlighted when you activate the bar. When you type one of these letters, you bring down a menu and see the commands that are on it. You enter commands in many DOS programs by choosing commands from menus on a menu bar.

4 Press **F** to drop down the File menu from the menu bar. You see the File menu commands on-screen. Each of these commands has a highlighted letter. If you press this letter on the keyboard, you choose the command and perform the action it specifies.

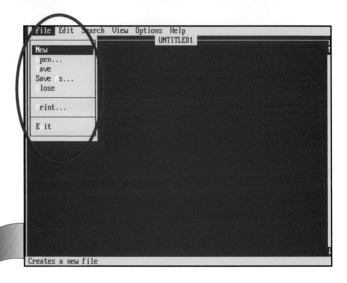

5 Press **X** to choose the Exit command. The application program closes, and the DOS prompt reappears.

6 At the DOS prompt, type **WIN** and press **Enter**. WIN is the command to start Windows 3.1. Windows loads into your computer's memory and appears on-screen. (If you have Windows 95, it started automatically when you started your computer.) ■

PART VIII

Using Your Computer

What Is Application Software?

Understanding an operating system is usually the most difficult part of dealing with a computer. Luckily, you don't have to use the DOS prompt very much any more—you can use Windows 95 to organize your system and software *applications* to do your work. Applications are the programs you use on your computer to accomplish specific tasks, such as write letters, set up a budget, or create a mailing list.

If you think of an operating system as a general contractor hired to control your PC worksite, then applications are the specialists that you call in to perform a particular service. Just as you call in a plumber to take care of installing a bathroom, your operating system calls in a word processing application to take care of typing.

THE CAPTAIN COOKIE FAN CLUB NEWSLETTER

Well, fans, the new season of The Captain Cookie Show starts next week, and reports out of Hollywood indicate that this will be the best one yet! If you're not tuned in on Saturday morning, you won't know what you're missing.

The first episode of the new season is MY CRUMBY FRIEND, during which Cap gets a new sidekick. Those of us who remember the last time the Crunchy Crusader got a sidekick know what a mistake that was. Luckily, they got rid of "Kid Cracker" after only three episodes, but those were three of the worst episodes in the entire run of the series! However, the producers promise us that the new sidekick, Snacky Sam, is nothing like K.C. While K.C. was constantly whining, never helping, and was held hostage in every single episode he was in, Snacky Sam is an industrious young cookie. Sure, Captain Cookie might have to save him from time to time, but then again, he'll have to save the Captain as well!

The second episode, THIS MAN, THIS MUNCHIE, brings back The Deadly Donut, one of our favorite villains. It sure looked like he was dead in his last appearance ("Donuts To You," the seventh episode of last season), but The Deadly Donut has come back from the dead several times before, so this comes as no surprise. What will come as a surprise is his voice; Paul Grant, who portrayed the character in all of his previous appearances, has retired from the microphone for health reasons. Replacing him is Carl Pietrantonio, who has provided the voice for Rasty Rusty and several members of the All-Evil Squad in the past, as well as being the title voice on The Adventures of Indy Ahnatko.

Also reappearing this season will be Doctor McMesmer, the Terrible Tucker Triplets, and everyone's favorite villainess, Jennifervor. There are no appearances planned for Leroy Lizard, though, partly because Kirk Quinn (who provided Leroy's voice) has gotten divorced from show producer Cheryl Miller.

In other cast notes, Murph Malone, who plays Cap's crusty butler, (continued on page 3)

Now the bad news: Because of rising costs, we're going to have to raise subscription rates by $2 per year. We will be giving you an extra issue per year for that money, however, and plan to make it a complete episode guide! More details will be sent with your renewal notice.

Last name: JOSEPHSON   First name: CHARLES
Address: 809 MONTANA AVE
City: RIVERTON   State: NJ   ZIP: 08083
Phone: (609) 555 - 8229
Number of orders: 13   Last order date: 12/17/93
Amount outstanding: $700   Due since: 01/10/94
Salesman: BILL

CLIENTS

Some of the most commonly used types of applications include:

- Word processors

- Spreadsheets

- Databases

- Graphics

- Desktop publishing

- Communications

NOTE ▼

The words *application*, *software*, and *program* are often used interchangeably.

Buying Applications

Before you buy software applications or programs, take some time to determine your needs. Ending up with a program that doesn't perform the way you expected is very frustrating, not to mention costly.

Here are some things you can do to help determine what kind of program is right for you:

- Make a list of the things you want to do with the program. Do you want to type letters? Set up a budget? Send out mass mailings? All three?

- Next, make a list of the things you might want to do in the future. For example, all you want to do today is type a form letter, but next month you might want to send out a newsletter.

- Set a budget for how much money you want to spend. Software programs vary in price, depending on how many features they offer, so you should have a price in mind.

- Shop around. Pick up a computer publication, and read the ads and the product reviews. Talk to friends and coworkers about their programs. Go into a software store and ask to see a demonstration.

After you decide on a program, make sure that it is compatible with your PC and vice versa. If you don't have a PC yet, make sure the PC you buy is compatible

> **NOTE** ▼
>
> If you haven't already purchased a PC, good! The best plan is to decide on the software you need, and then buy the right equipment to run that software.

with the software you want to use! Most software packages list the system requirements right on the box. System requirements tell you what hardware and software you must have in order to use the program. If you are still unsure of what you need, ask a salesperson or call the manufacturer.

Here are the things you should look for:

- Which microprocessors does the application require?

- How much memory do you need to run this program?

- How much disk space do you need to run this program?

- What versions of DOS does it require?

- What versions of Windows does it require?

- Is the application compatible with hardware, such as modems or sound cards, you already have?

- Does the application require additional hardware devices, such as a mouse or a modem?

- Does the application come with technical support or training?

- Can you return the application?

DOS versus Windows

Application programs need an operating system in order to work. If your PC has DOS, you can buy programs written to run on a DOS-based PC (this is indicated on the package). If you also have Windows 3.11, you can use Windows 3.11 applications and DOS applications, but not Windows 95 applications. If you have Windows 95, you can use applications written for DOS, Windows 3.11, or Windows 95.

Developers of Windows 3.11 and Windows 95 applications design the applications to make use of a standard Windows interface. Most Windows applications use the same menus, the same keystrokes, and the same commands to accomplish familiar tasks. That means that once you learn to use Windows, you can quickly learn to use just about every Windows application. Also, with most Windows applications, you can move and copy data from one program to another.

DOS applications are all different. You must learn to use each one individually, from scratch. DOS applications are not as graphically oriented or as intuitive as Windows applications. However, DOS applications generally require less memory and take up less disk space on your PC. They also usually run faster than Windows applications.

In general, if you have Windows 3.11, you buy Windows 3.11 applications, and you buy Windows 95 applications if you have Windows 95 (however, Windows 3.11 applications do run under Windows 95. They just don't take advantage of all of the Windows 95 features). If you already have DOS-based applications, you may be able to use them with either version of Windows, but they cannot take advantage of the Windows interface and other conveniences associated with Windows.

Software Suites

A software suite is a bundle, or group, of different compatible applications sold by one software company. The programs are each individual applications, but they usually work in a similar manner, and have some common features, such as menu commands, buttons, or keystrokes.

Although you can purchase each of the programs in a suite separately, when you purchase them as a bundle, they cost less. In addition, the manufacturer usually adds some features that make it easier to use them together.

Most software suites come with three or more common applications that you can use just as you would use a stand-alone package. Typically, a suite includes a word processor, a spreadsheet, and a database. Other packages that a suite may include are presentation graphics applications, personal information managers, and e-mail applications.

In addition, the applications the suites include are usually somewhat integrated with one another, making it easy to use them together and to transfer data from one into the others. For example, the applications may have a common menu that enables you to easily switch back and forth between applications.

Some of the features to consider when purchasing a software suite include:

- *A consistent interface* that the programs share so that you can easily learn to use them all.

- *Usefulness* of the programs to your needs. If you already have applications that you like, or if you do not need all of the programs in the suite, you might be better off buying each program separately.

- *Compatibility* between the different packages ensures that you can transfer data easily.

- *Level of integration* between the different packages is important if you want to be able to move from one to the other quickly and easily. Some manufacturers add menus or buttons that provide direct access to the other programs in the suite, so you do not have to use Windows to switch back and forth.

You benefit from using a software suite if you:

- Have not yet purchased any applications.

- Need to use the data from one application to accomplish tasks in another application.

- Want to use programs that are as similar as possible.

Some popular software suite packages include:

- Microsoft Office

- Lotus SmartSuite

- Borland WordPerfect Office

- Microsoft Works

- ClarisWorks

Word Processing

A *word processor* is just a computerized typewriter. You use it to enter, edit, arrange, and print text. You can use one to create memos, letters, reports, brochures...any printed material!

How You Use a Word Processing Application

All word processors are designed for producing different kinds of written documents. Some are simple—they have features for typing, editing, and printing. Some word processing programs are complex—they have features for formatting characters and pages, and for incorporating drawings, tables, and charts into documents.

You would benefit from using a word processor if you:

- Spend a lot of time typing and revising documents.

- Send out mailings.

- Write documents of any kind.

Some features to consider in a word processing package include:

- *Word wrap* feature that automatically wraps text from the end of one line to the beginning of the next line. If a word processing program has word wrap, it means you don't need to press Enter at the end of each line (unlike a typewriter, where you hit Return whenever you get to the end of a line). This makes it easy to insert or delete text. The word processing program automatically adjusts the line breaks.

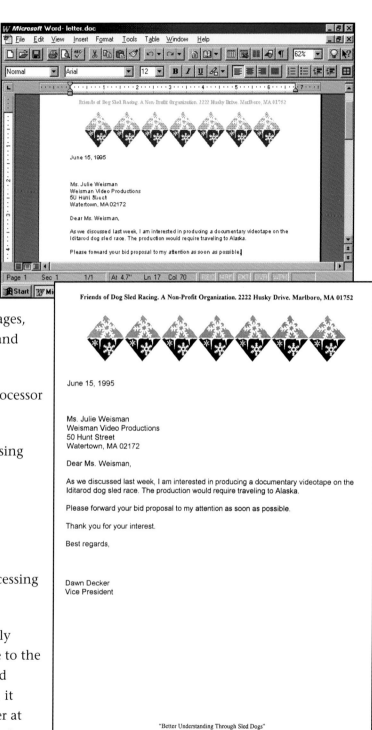

- Features that enable you to *copy* and *move* text from one place in a document to another, or to another document. This makes rearranging the text easy. *Drag and drop editing* enables you to accomplish these tasks using a mouse: you just select the text and drag it to its new place in the document.

- *Search and replace* features that help you look for a particular word or phrase within a document; if you want, you can replace all instances of a word, phrase, or type of formatting. Suppose that you use the name Smith throughout a document, and you find out that the correct spelling is Smythe. You just search for all instances of Smith and replace them with Smythe.

- *Formatting* features that enable you to dress up your text, paragraphs, and pages. Unlike a typewriter, a word processing program gives you more control over the look of a document. You can add emphasis-style attributes such as boldface, italic, and underline. You can change the font and the font size. You can even position paragraphs as you want them to appear on the page.

- *WYSIWYG* editing that enables you to see on-screen how the document looks when you print it. (WYSIWYG stands for "what-you-see-is-what-you-get.")

- For a poor typist or speller, a *spell check* feature that flags misspelled words and repeated words. You still need to proofread the document, however, because the spell check doesn't know whether you mean "to," "too," or "two."

- *Grammar checkers* that alert you about broken grammatical rules in your documents.

- If you send the same letter to lots of people, a word processing program with a *merge* feature that enables you to write form letters. Merging combines a mailing list with a form letter, creating a unique letter for each name on the mailing list.

- Features that enable you to create an *index* or *table of contents* automatically, create and rearrange an *outline* easily, mark *revisions*, or add *footnotes* and *endnotes*.

Popular Word Processors

Some popular word processing packages include:

- WordPerfect

- Microsoft Word

- WordPro

Spreadsheets

You use *spreadsheet* applications to manipulate numbers and compute mathematical equations. You can add, subtract, multiply, divide, and perform more advanced calculations on the numbers you enter. The difference between a spreadsheet and a calculator is that when you change a number in a spreadsheet, any formulas that use that number update automatically. No more totaling the numbers each time you make a change, as you do with a calculator!

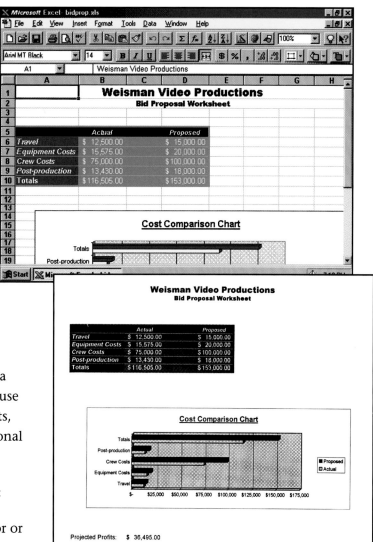

How You Use a Spreadsheet

Spreadsheets help you organize your data and analyze the results. You commonly use spreadsheets for creating financial reports, graphs and charts, and for tracking personal finances.

You will find a spreadsheet useful if you:

- Spend a lot of time with a calculator or adding machine.

- Prepare financial reports of any kind.

- Like to play around with numbers.

Some features to consider in a spreadsheet package include:

- *Formulas* and built-in *functions* (predefined formulas) that you can use to set up and perform common calculations. Most spreadsheets include functions for calculating loan payments, computing averages, and compounding interest.

- *What-If* analysis that enables you to see what the results would be if you changed certain data. For example, you can consider what would happen to profits if you raise the price of a product by 10 percent.

- *Graphing and charting* features that enable you to use pictures to show trends or overall relationships between numbers. A pie chart of sales by product, for example, shows how much each product contributes to the total amount of sales.

- *Formatting* features that enable you to display numbers as dollar values, percentages, or dates, and position text, use different fonts, and add effects such as shading or borders.

Popular Spreadsheet Programs

Some popular spreadsheet packages include:

- Lotus 1-2-3

- Microsoft Excel

- Quattro Pro

Databases

A *database* application stores, tracks, and manages records of any kind of information you enter into the PC. Most database programs have two parts: one part is like a giant Rolodex file that you fill with electronic index cards; the other part is like a research assistant you can tell to search through the records, sort them according to the criteria you specify, and generate reports.

Some database programs are powerful, and difficult to use, rivaling programming languages in their complexity. If you need a program that offers straightforward data storage and retrieval, look for one that falls into the category of *personal information managers* (PIMs). PIMs are generally less sophisticated than some full-blown database programs, yet they provide plenty of features for organizing and analyzing data.

How You Use a Database

With a database program, you collect, organize, and analyze information. You can keep track of employees, mailing lists, recipes, clients, and a vast range of other data. Once you enter the information into the database, you can use it in many ways. With a database of clients, for example, you can create a mailing list, generate a form letter, or quickly identify whom you should call when you travel to Phoenix next month.

You will find a database program useful if you:

- Keep records of any kind.

- Use records to assemble lists or reports.

Some features to consider in a database package include:

- A *search* or *find* feature that enables you to scan through the records in the database to find the information you need.

- *Sorting* that enables you to organize and arrange the records within the database.

- *Query* functions that specify the information you want the database to search or sort. For instance, you might want to compile a list of all entries with a certain ZIP code.

- *Built-in reports* that enable you to organize the information from the records for analysis or distribution.

Relational versus Flat-File Databases

There are two basic kinds of database programs: relational and flat-file.

In a *relational database*, you can relate or combine the information you enter in one database file with the information from another database file. This is useful for large, complex projects that require information from many sources.

In a *flat-file database*, you cannot relate or combine information from different files with records from other database files.

To decide which type you need, you must consider how you use your current records. For example, if you need reports that combine information from your client "Rolodex" with information from your employee "Rolodex," you probably need a relational database.

Popular Database Programs

Some popular database packages include:

■ Borland dBASE

■ Lotus Approach

■ Microsoft Access

■ Microsoft FoxPro

■ Borland Paradox

Graphics

You use graphics applications to create artwork that you print or incorporate into other applications, such as desktop publishing packages and word processing programs. You can use graphics software to create simple line drawings, complex schematics, charts, or presentations.

How You Use Graphics Programs

There are different kinds of graphics programs, all designed to help you create drawings and illustrations that you can use for different purposes. Some of the basic categories of graphics programs include:

■ *Clip art* programs that come with pre-drawn artwork that you can simply copy into any document.

■ *Draw* and *paint* programs that have the tools you need to create your own artwork.

■ *Computer-aided design* (CAD) programs, sophisticated versions of draw and paint packages, that you use to create detailed images, such as schematics and blueprints. CAD programs often include 3-D imaging.

■ *Presentation graphics* programs that come with the tools you need to develop presentations on slides or overhead transparencies.

You will find a graphics program useful if you:

■ Create documents that you can improve with artwork.

■ Create artwork that you use independently.

■ Design models of anything—including gardens, interior designs, skyscrapers, and airliners.

■ Develop presentations for any purpose.

Some of the features you should consider in a graphics package include:

- *Drawing tools* that select the method you use for creating an image. With some tools you draw freehand; others create perfect geometric shapes, or add text to an image. Tools also determine the effects you can achieve, such as a paintbrush effect or a spray-can effect.

- *Image editing* features that enable you to modify a drawing without starting over. You should be able to erase a part of the image, move a piece, or change the color of a part without changing the rest.

- *3-D imaging* that enables you to view an object on-screen from different angles.

- *Compatibility* with other programs. This is important if you want to save the image in a file you can use with another application, or create slides or images from data you already entered in a spreadsheet, database, or word processing program.

Popular Graphics Programs

Some popular graphics programs include:

- Harvard Graphics

- Animator

- CorelDRAW!

- AutoCAD

- PowerPoint

- Paint

- Generic CADD

- Freelance Graphics

Desktop Publishing

You use desktop publishing applications to create documents that look typeset like professional publications.

Usually, desktop publishing applications combine data from other applications, such as text from a word processor and artwork from a graphics package. You can even include scanned images such as photographs or line art in desktop-published documents.

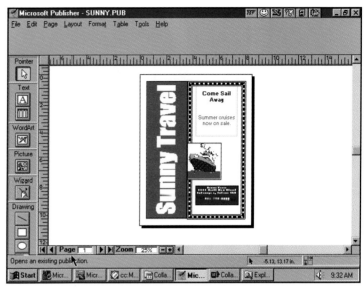

How You Use a Desktop Publishing Application

You use a desktop publishing application to create newsletters, reports, books, annual reports, and any other document that may require page layout.

Although some word processing programs include simple desktop publishing features, true desktop publishing programs can be very complex and powerful.

You will find a desktop publishing program useful if you:

- Produce documents for publication, such as reports and newsletters.

- Want to incorporate graphics in your documents.

- Find a word processing program too limiting in its page layout and document design functions.

Some features to consider in a desktop publishing package include:

- *Page formatting* that sets margins, headers, footers, columns, and other page design features.

- *Templates* that save a page layout for use in other documents.

- *Text editing* that enables you to make changes to text, set fonts and styles, and move and position text on a page.

- *Graphics capabilities* that enable you to create and change artwork, and move and position images on a page.

- *Built-in fonts* that give your printed materials a unique and original appearance.

- *Compatibility* that enables you to work with other applications is necessary if you want to use the files from your word processing application or the artwork from your graphics package. Also, find out if you can use fonts from other packages, or scanned images.

Popular Desktop Publishing Programs

Popular desktop publishing programs include:

- Adobe PageMaker

- Corel Ventura

- Microsoft Publisher

- PFS: First Publisher

Communications

If your PC is equipped with a modem and communications software, you can explore the wonderful world of online communications. You can exchange information, messages, and ideas with millions of people around the world who also have PCs equipped with a modem and communications software.

In addition to direct PC to PC communications, which you can accomplish simply by telling your modem to dial the phone number of the other PC's modem, many online services help people connect with other people.

To use a communications program, you need a modem and a telephone line.

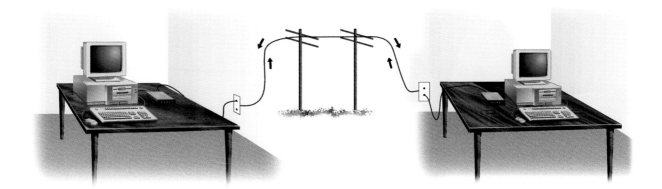

How You Use a Communications Program

The basic purpose of communications programs is to control the way your computer transmits and receives data. Most programs also store a directory of telephone numbers, automatically dial calls, and save communications settings.

You will find communications software useful if you:

- Exchange data regularly with a computer at a different location, such as a computer at a main office or corporate headquarters.

- Want to send e-mail to someone not connected to the same PC network that you are connected to.

- Are interested in accessing online services, such as CompuServe, America Online, Prodigy, GEnie, or the Microsoft Network.

- Want to look at the vast amount of information available via the global network of computers known as the Internet.

Some features to consider in a communications application include:

- *Telephone directories* that store a list of telephone numbers that you dial frequently.

- *Automatic dialers* that dial the number you enter in the telephone directory. This feature saves you the trouble of entering the same numbers again and again.

- *Automatic answerers* that tell the modem to answer incoming calls.

- Built-in *error correction* that checks files for errors as you send and receive the files. There are different error-correction standards, so make sure that you get one you can use with your modem.

- Built-in *data compression* compresses or decompresses data as you send or receive it, so that it takes less time to send the data. Several data-compression standards exist, so make sure that you get one you can use with your modem. Just ask your supplier, or read the documentation, to make sure that you have the correct one.

- *File transfer protocols* that help ensure that you exchange data without errors. There are many different protocols available, and you must use the same one at both ends of the communications link.

- *Graphics* support that enables you to send or receive files stored in a non-text, or graphics, format.

- *E-mail* support that enables you to type messages in *real time* (while you are sitting at your PC connected to another computer) to another computer. You do not have to store the message in a file in order to transmit it.

Popular Communications Programs

Some popular communications programs include:

- ProComm Plus

- CrossTalk

- Delrina WinComm

- HyperTerminal (which comes free with Windows 95)

- Qmodem Pro

- PCTalk

NOTE ▼

Although, e-mail, online services, and bulletin boards facilitate communications between computer users, they are not technically communications software. You do, however, have to have a communications program before you can access Internet e-mail, online services, and bulletin boards.

Electronic Mail, or E-Mail

E-mail is an application that enables you to send public or private messages to other computer users on a network, an online service, or a bulletin board. E-mail support may be built into communications software, or built into other applications designed for use on a network. Usually, the e-mail program stores the messages on the network until the user wants to read them.

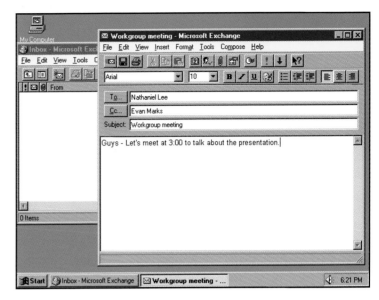

How You Use E-Mail

There are many different kinds of e-mail systems, but they all provide the same basic services for sending and retrieving messages, and attaching files to messages. Usually, you can print e-mail messages, store them for future reference, or simply read messages and delete them.

Addressing E-Mail

To send an e-mail message, you must address it to the person you want to receive it. On your company's network, that may be as simple as typing the person's name or ID.

Every person using online service e-mail systems—such as CompuServe Mail or MCI Mail—or Internet e-mail has an address. Since thousands of people use these services, and each person must have a unique address, the addresses can look rather cryptic. Often, they include lots of numbers, letters, and symbols, such as dots (.) and the at sign (@).

When you send mail to someone via the Internet you need to include not only the individual's ID, but also the address of the online service or Internet site—called the *domain*—where the individual's mail box is located. The address is read from right to left. The last three letters identify the kind of place the message is coming from (.com—a business or online service, .edu—a university or educational institution, .org— an organization); the word or numbers before that are the account number or name of the person sending the message, in one format or another. Here are a few sample Internet e-mail addresses:

Sample Internet E-Mail Addresses

Address	Is Sent to
johnson@host.sleddog.org	someone whose ID is johnson, at a computer named host, at an organization called sleddog.
21111.112@compuserve.com	someone who has an account with the CompuServe online service with the ID number 21111,112.
johnson123@aol.com	someone who belongs to the America Online online service and whose ID is johnson.

Some of the features to consider in an e-mail package:

- An *address book* that enables you to store the names and e-mail addresses of people you communicate with frequently

- The ability to *broadcast* messages to more than one person, to everyone in a workgroup, or to everyone on the network

- *Remote access* that enables you to call in from remote locations to retrieve your e-mail messages using a PC equipped for communications.

You would benefit from using e-mail if you:

- Are part of a workgroup that collaborates on projects or ideas.

- Travel frequently but need to communicate with others at home or at work.

- Enjoy communicating with others via online services or the Internet.

Popular Network E-Mail Programs

The following are some of the most popular programs you can use to send e-mail:

- Microsoft Mail

- Lotus cc:Mail

- Microsoft Exchange

- Most of the popular online services offer e-mail systems and access to the Internet e-mail system.

Online Services and the Internet

One of the most popular uses for a personal computer is accessing online services and the Internet. If you have a modem, a phone line, and communications software, for a monthly fee, you can subscribe to an online communications service, such as CompuServe, America Online, Prodigy, Microsoft Network, or GEnie.

When you subscribe to an online service, you pay a monthly fee for basic services, and a premium, or hourly fee, for additional services. You dial a local telephone number, and your modem connects you through a bank of modems to a central computer, which in turn connects you to the service you want to use. Depending on your personal telephone service, you may also have to pay additional telephone charges.

The Internet is a world-wide communications system comprised of tens of millions of computers linked together in a vast network. Originally, government agencies and educational institutions supported the Internet, but access to the Internet has expanded and has grown increasingly more public over time. Currently, the Internet provides millions of people with access to information on every topic under the sun.

How You Use the Internet

Using online services as a gateway to the Internet, you can tap into information all over the world, including stock quotes and weather conditions, as well as to products and services, including banking, retail shopping, and airline reservation systems. You can send and receive private messages with other PC users who subscribe to any service or work for a company with access to the Internet. Also, you can play the most current games, and you can join user groups and engage in typed conversations with other people who are on the system at the same time. Since most media organizations have Internet access, you can submit letters to the editors of newspapers and magazines. You can communicate with people at colleges and universities, your senator or representative, and your favorite musicians and movie stars.

Some of the features to consider when subscribing to an online service include:

- *Monthly fees* that usually provide access to basic services, but not to premium services. Find out exactly what you get for your monthly fee, and how much additional services cost.

- An *e-mail* allotment that permits you to send a certain amount of e-mail for free each month. After that, you must pay to send messages, usually according to the size of the message.

- A *user interface* that may be a blank screen with single lines of text, or a Windows-compatible graphical interface with menus, icons, and button bars. Make sure you are comfortable with the interface before you subscribe to the service.

- *Internet access* that provides you with a direct link to the Internet.

- *Customer support*, especially if you are new to the world of online services. Find out if you can get help online, or if you can call someone for support. Some subscriptions include monthly magazines with information about new services, pricing, and helpful hints.

Communicating Online

Communicating online has its own little quirks. For example, to overcome the problem of how to convey emotion on-line, e-mail users have developed *emoticons*—little pictures you can type using the standard keyboard. Also, many users communicate with a form of shorthand that makes it easier to type common expressions. Perhaps the most important rule is to avoid typing a message in all capital letters. Using all caps is the online equivalent of shouting, and people will tell you that you are being rude!

Here's a quick guide to help you understand why acronyms you've never seen before, as well as parentheses and commas in strange configurations, fill your messages:

Emoticon or shorthand	Meaning
:-)	Smile
:-D	Big Smile
:-(	Frown
;-)	Wink
<G>	Grin
BRB	Be right back
IMO	In my opinion
ROTFL	Rolling on the floor laughing
TIA	Thanks in advance

Almost everyone benefits from an online service or Internet access. For example, you benefit if you:

- Enjoy communicating with a wide variety of people all over the world on a wide variety of topics.

- Want access to electronic services such as banking, stock prices, and mail-order retail sales.

- Conduct research that requires gathering information from a lot of different sources and locations.

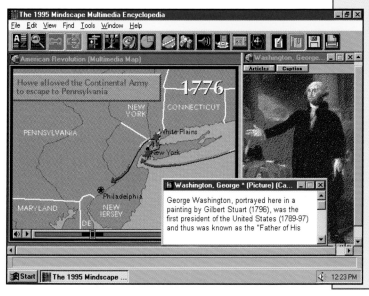

Multimedia Applications

With multimedia applications, you can generate sound, video, animation, graphics, and text. Multimedia brings life to the traditionally dull, text-based world of personal computing. With multimedia applications, a CD-ROM drive, a sound card, and speakers, you can enter a multi-dimensional world of education and entertainment.

Multimedia applications are available on CD-ROMs, so you must have a CD-ROM drive attached to your PC in order to run multimedia applications.

How You Use Multimedia Applications

You use most multimedia applications to play games or for educational purposes. For example, if you use a multimedia encyclopedia, you not only read information about what you look up, but also you can see what something looks like and hear how it sounds. Multimedia games are more life-like than other games, providing live-action video and real-life sound effects.

Kids and adults alike enjoy controlling the action in story and movie plots with multimedia books and videos. You can also use multimedia applications to play and record music and video and to travel to places you've never been before.

You will enjoy multimedia applications if you:

- Like to play action games on your PC.

- Like to hear music and other sounds.

- Use research materials frequently.

Some features to consider in a multimedia application include:

- *Compatibility* with your PC. It must work with your CD-ROM drive and your sound cards. If you want to record music, you must have a musical device that conforms to the MIDI standard, and if you want to capture video, you must have a video capture board.

- *Graphics* that make the multimedia application exciting and fun to use. Make sure the quality is worth the price.

- *Entertaining* multimedia applications—just because it's on a CD-ROM doesn't mean it's going to be fun. Read reviews and ask your friends before buying a program.

Popular Multimedia Applications

Some popular multimedia applications include:

- Microsoft Encarta 95 (an encyclopedia)

- Grolier's Multimedia Encyclopedia

- Compton's Interactive Encyclopedia

- Software Toolworks World Atlas and Software Toolworks U.S. Atlas

- Myst (a game)

- SimCity 2000 (a simulator for building cities)

- Oregon Trail (a game)

Other Applications

There are too many types of applications to count or to list here. Someone has written a program for pretty much anything you can imagine doing with a computer.

Here are some examples of other software applications you may be interested in:

- With *financial programs* you perform finance-related tasks such as creating tax returns, balancing your checkbook, and setting up an accounting system. Quicken is one of the most widely used personal finance programs.

- *Utility programs* enhance a computer system by helping you manage your hardware and software. Many packages come with built-in utilities. DOS 6.22, for example, comes with a utility for backing up disks, and Windows 95 comes with utilities that perform such tasks as checking for viruses and creating backups of data.

- *Personal Information Managers* help you organize your life. You can use them to store information about business contacts, set your daily schedule, and prioritize your work.

- *Educational programs* enable users of all ages and in all subjects to learn about typing, spelling, reading, and planning a travel route.

- *Games* are for fun. They, too, enable users of all ages and in all subjects to play card games, golf, baseball, war games, and flight simulation.

To get an idea of the possibilities, look through some computer software catalogs, or browse through a software store.

Software Installation

When you purchase a software program, it comes on floppy disks or on CD-ROM. You must *install* the program, usually onto your hard disk, before you can use it. You cannot just put the program's floppy disks or CD in the disk drive, or copy the files from the floppy disk onto a hard disk.

Most programs come with an installation program and instructions. Read the instructions carefully before you install the program. You may need to know certain information about your PC, such as the kind and model of printer you have, or to which port you connected the printer. Or, you may discover that the installation disk is a $3^1/_2$-inch floppy disk, and you have a $5^1/_4$-inch disk drive.

Application Software Troubleshooting Checklist

If you encounter problems while using a software application, take the following steps:

1. Watch to see if the disk drive in-use lights are flashing. You may think the program is not responding, when it is just taking a long time to process your most recent command.

2. If your computer displays an error message, write it down. Look in the user's manual for information about the message, and have it with you when you call the customer support line.

3. Press F1, or the appropriate Help function key, to see if a help screen is available.

4. If something displays on the screen that you did not expect, press the Esc key once or twice. Usually, the Esc key cancels the current action and returns you to where you were before.

5. If the computer is hung up and does not respond to anything you do, press Ctrl, Alt, and Del at the same time to restart the computer. *All data left in RAM will be lost.*

When you are ready, find the installation instructions in the program documentation and follow the installation instructions carefully. When you have completely installed the program, put the original floppy disks in a safe place and send in the product registration card.

Glossary

3½-inch disk   A floppy disk enclosed in a hard, plastic case. These disks come in two capacities: double density (720K) and high density (1.44M or 2.88M).

5¼-inch disk   A floppy disk enclosed in a flexible, plastic case. These disks come in two capacities: double density (360K) and high density (1.2M).

access time   The average time it takes for a hard or floppy disk drive to find and read information from a disk.

accessory   A utility program included with Windows 95 that you can use in conjunction with other programs. For example, Paint and WordPad are accessory programs. These programs are sometimes called "applets."

acoustic modem   A modem that connects to the phone handset instead of to the phone line.

address   The location where something is stored in the computer's memory. Also, a specific device or location on a network.

America Online   A popular on-line service company.

applets   Another name for the accessory programs that come with Windows 95, including Paint and WordPad.

application   A software program designed to help you perform a specific task. Word processors and spreadsheets are two common types of application programs.

ASCII   An acronym for American Standard Code for Information Interchange. It's a standard text format that you use for text-only files.

AUTOEXEC.BAT   A file that DOS reads and processes each time you start a PC. It usually includes commands that control the way the computer runs.

back up   To copy the files from a hard disk to a removable storage medium, such as floppy disk or tape. The copied files are called backups.

background computing   A feature that allows the computer to perform a function, such as printing or formatting, while the computer processes another application on-screen.

batch file   A file that contains a series of DOS commands. The computer executes the commands when you run the batch file. You may use DOS to create a batch file that makes a certain directory current and starts a program.

baud rate   The speed at which a modem transmits data. Baud rate is measured in bits per second (bps).

BBS   See *bulletin board service*.

BIOS   An acronym for Basic Input/Output System. The BIOS is a program that controls communication between the CPU and input/output devices.

bit   The smallest unit of information; eight bits make up a byte. Also, the memory or disk space used to store that information.

boot   To start a computer and load the operating system.

BPS   An abbreviation for bits per second (bit/sec), it is the measurement unit for communication speed.

Briefcase   An accessory program that comes with Windows 95. It enables you to transport files between a laptop computer and a desktop PC, making sure that the latest version of each file is on both computers.

browser   Software that provides an easy-to-use interface to sites on the Internet or World Wide Web.

bulletin board service (BBS)   A computer that is set up to receive and distribute messages over a modem.

bus   A set of wires or conductors that carry signals between the different internal computer components.

byte   A measure of information stored on a disk. One byte equals eight bits (just about one character).

cache An area of fast memory that the CPU uses to store the information it uses a lot. Caches help the CPU run faster.

capacity The amount of data that can be stored on a disk or in memory. Capacity is measured in bytes, kilobytes (K), megabytes (M), and gigabytes (G).

CD-ROM An acronym for Compact Disk, Read-Only Memory. CD-ROMs are storage devices that contain large amounts of data (more than 600 megabytes).

CD-ROM drive A device used by the PC to read data from CD-ROMs.

central processing unit (CPU) The main microprocessor chip that controls the computer; in other words, the brain of the computer. The CPU is stored inside the system unit.

CGA An acronym for Computer Graphics Array, which is an old, low-quality standard for video adapters.

chip A tiny, integrated circuit that either controls computer functions or stores information. The microprocessor, math coprocessor, and read-only memory storage units are chips.

click To press and release a mouse button.

clients Computers on a local area network that receive files from the LAN file server.

clip art A collection of graphics files that you can buy for use with word processing, graphics, and desktop publishing applications.

Clipboard A feature of Windows that enables you to copy or move text and graphics from one document to another. In Windows 95, it enables you to copy or move files from one folder or disk to another.

clone An IBM PC-compatible computer built by another manufacturer.

cold boot Starting a computer by turning it on with the power switch. See also *warm boot*.

command An instruction the user or program gives to the computer.

COMMAND.COM An essential DOS file that contains the command processor.

compatibility The capability of one computer to run the software of another. Also, the capability of different hardware components to work together.

CompuServe A popular on-line service company.

computer A machine that processes information.

computer-aided design (CAD) Application programs that people such as engineers use to design physical objects.

CONFIG.SYS A special DOS file that determines the way your computer runs. DOS executes the commands in this file every time it starts.

continuous-feed paper Perforated computer paper that runs through the sprockets on impact printers so that paper is always available. Also called tractor-feed or fan-fold paper.

conventional memory All of the random-access memory in a PC up to 640K.

CPU See *central processing unit.*

current Describes an item that is being used by the computer at that moment. For example, the open folder is the current folder. The document you are working in is the current document. Also called active.

cursor A marker used to indicate the current position of input or output on a monitor display.

data Any kind of information a computer processes or stores.

data file A computer file that stores information that a software program uses.

database An application that stores and retrieves related sets of information. For example, a database can store a mailing list.

defragment To reorganize files on a disk into consecutive blocks as opposed to fragmented blocks. This typically improves the speed and efficiency with which data is accessed.

density A term that describes the amount of information you can store on a disk. Double-density disks store 360K or 720K of data; high-density disks store 1.2M, 1.44M, or 2.88M of data.

desktop A type of system unit case that fits conveniently on the top of a desk.

Desktop In Windows 95, the initial screen that contains icons that represent My Computer, Network Neighborhood, Recycle Bin, Briefcase, Inbox, frequently used files, and any shortcuts you may have defined.

desktop publishing program An application that combines text formatting and graphics manipulation to create professional-looking documents.

device driver   A program that helps your computer communicate with the equipment attached to it, such as the printer or the mouse.

dialog box   A window that opens on-screen. A dialog box either provides information about the current action or asks you to enter additional information to complete the current action.

digitizing tablet   A hardware device you use to input artwork into your computer by drawing on it with a stylus.

directory   A grouping of files and other directories on a hard disk. Also called a folder.

directory tree   The organizational structure of directories on a disk.

disk   A device that a computer uses for storing information. See also *hard disk* and *floppy disk.*

disk drive   A hardware device that reads and writes information to and from magnetic storage disks. Disk drive types include hard disk drives, floppy disk drives, and CD-ROMs.

docking station   A component that enables you to use a portable computer as a desktop system.

DOS   An acronym for Disk Operating System. DOS is a common PC operating system. It manages the PC's resources, including files, disks, and programs.

DOS prompt   The user interface that appears on-screen when DOS is waiting for a command. Minimally, the DOS prompt displays the current drive like this: A:\> or C:\>.

dot pitch   The distance between the pixels (or the tiny dots that make up your screen display) on a color monitor.

dot-matrix printer   An impact printer that arranges dots in rows and columns to print text and graphics on a page.

double density   A measurement of disk capacity. A $3^1/_2$-inch double-density floppy disk holds 720K, whereas a $5^1/_4$-inch floppy holds 360K. See also *high density.*

double-click   The act of pressing and releasing a mouse button twice in rapid succession.

double-speed   A CD-ROM drive that spins a disk twice as quickly as older, single-speed CD-ROM drives. Also called double-spin.

download   To transfer files from one computer to another using a modem.

dpi   An acronym for dots per inch, which is a measurement of image resolution.

drag   The act of pressing and holding down a mouse button and sliding the mouse pointer to another location, thereby moving an object (such as an icon) from one place to another.

Draw   An application you use to draw computer graphics.

drop   The act of releasing the mouse button after completing a drag.

e-mail   Electronic messages that you transmit to other computer users on a network or by way of a modem and an information service or a bulletin board service.

EGA   An acronym for Enhanced Graphics Adapter, which is a medium-quality standard for video adapters. This adapter is no longer available, but may exist on older monitors.

EISA   An acronym for Extended Industry Standard Architecture, which is a standard design for system buses.

electronic mail   See *e-mail.*

emoticons   Combinations of keystrokes used to draw pictures that express emotions in e-mail messages. For example, :-) (view sideways) indicates that the person writing the e-mail is happy or joking.

ergonomic   A machine or tool that is designed for comfort and ease-of-use and to prevent injury.

escape   The act of pressing the Esc key. You use escape to cancel the current action.

expandability   The amount of room available in a computer for adding peripherals or memory.

expanded memory   A combination of hardware and software that tricks some computers and programs into accessing more than 1M of memory.

expansion card   A printed circuit board that fits into an expansion slot in the system unit for controlling peripherals or adding memory. Also called an expansion board.

expansion slot   A slot on the motherboard where you attach an expansion card.

Explorer   A feature of Windows 95 that enables you to display the contents of your disks and directories in a directory tree format. Similar to the File Manager in Windows 3.X.

extended memory   Memory above 1M used by PCs based on 80286, 80386, or 80486 microprocessors.

external modem   A modem that you attach to a PC using cables. An external modem is located outside rather than inside the system unit.

FAT   An acronym for file allocation table. Disks create this table during formatting for use in locating files.

fax   Short for facsimile. A way of transmitting data over phone lines. Faxing sends a hard copy or electronic copy of a document to a printer on the other end of the phone line.

file   A collection of data that a disk stores for future use. For example, a disk can store a letter or a worksheet as a file.

file allocation table   See *FAT*.

file extension   In DOS, three characters following a dot (.) at the end of a file or directory name. You don't need to worry about file extensions in Windows 95.

File Manager   Part of the Windows 3.X GUI that you use to control your files. Windows 95 replaces this with the Windows Explorer.

file name   The name you give a file so that you and your operating system can find the file on the disk.

file server   A computer that controls files, programs, and access on a local area network.

file specification   The complete name and path to a disk file. The file specification tells your operating system where to find the file.

file transfer protocol (FTP)   A program used to transfer files across the Internet. Also, a set of rules (or protocol) used by UNIX computers for transferring files.

fixed disk   See *hard disk*.

flatbed scanner   An automatic scanning device similar to a copy machine that you use to input written or printed data into a computer.

floppy disk   A removable magnetic device you use to store computer files. Also called a disk, a floppy, or a diskette.

floppy disk drive   A device that reads and writes information on a floppy disk.

font   A specific size and style of character that a PC prints or displays on-screen.

footprint   The amount of space a computer takes up on the desktop.

format   The process that prepares a disk for use. Also, the layout of information on a page, or, the particular way a PC stores data. For example, a PC stores graphics files in a graphics format, and text files in a text format.

forum   An on-line discussion of a specific topic among users of the CompuServe on-line service.

function keys   The keys on a PC keyboard labeled with the letter F and a number from 1 to 15 (some keyboards have fewer function keys). Function keys perform tasks or execute commands specific to the current application.

gigabyte (G)   One billion bytes.

graphical user interface (GUI)   An easy-to-use system of graphics, menus, and plain English commands that enable the user to communicate with the PC.

graphics accelerator   A video adapter the computer uses to increase the processing speed for displaying information on the monitor.

graphics adapter   See *video adapter*.

gray scale   The different shades of gray that a scanner translates into computer data.

GUI   An abbreviation for graphical user interface. You pronounce it "gooey."

hand scanner   A hand-held device you use to transfer information and pictures from hard copy to computer files.

hard copy   Printed information. Hard copy is sometimes called computer printout.

hard disk   A data storage device that is usually fixed inside the system unit. Hard disks range in size from 20M to over 500M bytes.

hardware   The physical parts of the computer that you see and touch. For example, the keyboard, the monitor, and the case that houses the system unit are all hardware.

high density   A measurement of disk capacity. $3^1/_2$-inch high-density floppy disks hold 1.44M or 2.88M of information, whereas $5^1/_4$-inch high-density floppies hold 1.2M. See also *double density*.

home page   A screenful of information about a particular site on the World Wide Web. Often allows access to additional information via hypertext links.

hypertext   Data that provides links to other related data, enabling you to jump from one document or topic to another related document or topic by simply clicking on a highlighted word. Application Help files and World Wide Web home pages use hypertext.

Hz   An abbreviation for hertz, which is a measurement of cycles per second.

icon   A picture that the graphical user interface uses to represent an element within the program. In Microsoft Windows, some common icons represent files, disks, and programs.

input   Data put into the computer for processing, usually when the user types information or presses a mouse button.

interface   A point of communication between parts of the PC, or between the user and the PC.

internal modem   A modem that connects to the computer in an expansion slot inside the system unit.

Internet   A vast world-wide network of computer networks. The Internet provides access to vast quantities of information on many topics.

I/O   An abbreviation for input/output.

I/O controller   The device that controls how the computer passes information through the I/O ports.

I/O device   A peripheral device that exchanges information with the computer, such as a keyboard or mouse.

I/O ports   Sockets on the computer that connect I/O devices to the computer.

ISA   An acronym for Industry Standard Architecture, which is a standard design for a system bus.

joystick   A pointing or input device you use mostly to play computer games.

keyboard   An input device you use to enter data or commands by typing.

kilobyte (K)   1,024 bytes. 1K is usually rounded to equal one thousand bytes. Kilobytes are used to measure disk capacity and memory.

LAN   See *local area network*.

laptop   A small, portable computer, which can weigh as little as six pounds. Laptops are popular with business travelers, who use them to get work done while they are away from the office.

laser printer   A non-impact printer that uses a laser beam and toner ink to create an image on paper.

local area network (LAN)   A group of computers linked by cables in a small area, such as one office building.

local bus   A direct connection between the CPU and the computer's RAM and other devices.

long file names   A feature of Windows 95 that enables you to create file names with more than the eight characters DOS limits you to.

math coprocessor   A computer chip that performs complex calculations. The microprocessor or the motherboard contains the math coprocessor. Graphics programs and programs that do many calculations use this coprocessor.

MCA   An acronym for Micro Channel Architecture, a type of PC bus.

megabyte (M)   One million bytes.

memory   The electronic circuitry where a PC stores information that it is not currently using.

microprocessor   The main chip that contains all the elements of the PC's central processing unit.

Microsoft Windows 3.1   An operating environment Microsoft Corporation developed for use with DOS. Windows uses a graphical user interface to simplify using a PC.

Microsoft Windows 95   A 32-bit operating system Microsoft Corporation developed for personal computers that combines a graphical user interface with operating system capabilities. Windows 95 replaces Windows 3.1.

modem   A device that transmits data over telephone lines. Short for MOdulator/DEModulator.

monitor   The hardware that displays the information you type on the keyboard and the PC's response to commands. The monitor also is called a display or screen.

motherboard   The main circuit board in the system unit. It usually holds the CPU, the RAM, and expansion boards.

mouse   A pointing device some programs use to input data.

mouse pad   A rubber pad that provides a uniform surface for a mouse to slide on.

mouse pointer   The symbol that indicates the location of the mouse on-screen.

MS-DOS   A version of DOS that was developed by Microsoft Corporation.

multimedia   Applications that use a combination of graphics, text, sound, and video, usually on CD-ROM.

multitasking   The capability of running more than one application at the same time.

My Computer   An icon on the Windows 95 desktop that provides visual access to the components connected to your PC.

nanosecond   About one billionth of a second.

network   A group of computers linked together by cables to share data and resources.

network interface card (NIC)   An expansion card that enables you to attach your PC to a network.

Network Neighborhood   An icon on the Windows 95 desktop that provides access to other computers on the same network.

notebook   A portable PC small enough to fit in a briefcase.

on-line   In regards to a hardware device, the state of being turned on. Also refers to the active exchange of data via computer.

operating system   A group of software programs that provides the instructions you need to control a PC.

OS/2   A PC operating system, marketed by IBM.

output   Data that the computer processes and returns to a format (on-screen or printed) the user can understand.

Paint   A Windows 95 accessory program used for creating and modifying graphic images.

parallel port   A type of port on the system unit you use to attach printers.

path   The route that the operating system must follow to find a disk file. Usually, a path includes the disk drive, all directories between the root directory and the file, and the complete file name.

PC   An acronym for personal computer. Usually, PC refers to an IBM-compatible personal computer.

Pentium   The name of a microprocessor chip Intel Corp. developed. The Pentium processor is currently the most advanced processor available for PCs.

peripherals   Hardware devices you attach to the main system unit. A printer, modem, and mouse are all peripherals.

pixel   A unit of measurement. Each pixel is one of many dots on the screen that forms displayed information. Short for *picture element.*

Plug-and-Play   The quality of some devices such as modems and sound cards to function as soon as you attach them to the computer. These devices do not require extensive setup and installation procedures.

point   The act of moving the mouse pointer so that it touches the desired element on-screen. Also a measure of type size (72 points equal one inch).

port   An electrical socket on the outside of the system unit that connects external peripherals to expansion cards on the inside of the system unit. Most PCs come with at least one parallel port, one serial port, one game port, and one video adapter port.

portable   A small PC that you can carry easily. Often, a portable runs on batteries. Different types of portables include notebooks and laptops.

POST   An acronym for Power On Self Test, which is a series of checks that the computer runs during startup to make sure everything is working right.

PostScript   The name of a printer control language that is a standard for graphics printing.

Prodigy   A popular on-line service company.

program   A set of instructions that tells the computer what to do. Also called *application* or *software.*

program group   In Microsoft Windows 3.X, a program group is a collection of related programs.

Program Manager   Part of the Windows 3.1 GUI that you use to start other programs.

protocol   The language that sets the rules for communication between hardware devices.

quad-speed   A CD-ROM drive that spins disks four times faster than single-speed drives. Most new computers with CD-ROM drives have quad-speed drives.

RAM An acronym for random-access memory. RAM is the electronic memory where the computer stores information until the computer needs it or stores it on a disk.

RAM disk An area of RAM that emulates a disk drive.

Recycle Bin A feature of Windows 95 that stores deleted files until you "empty" the bin. You can restore files from the Recycle Bin up until you empty the bin.

resolution A measurement of the quality or the sharpness of a monitor, the image on a monitor, or a printed image. Resolution usually is measured by the number of dots used to make the image.

ROM An acronym for read-only memory. ROM is memory that you cannot erase or add to. ROM provides the instructions that the computer needs to start each time you turn it on.

root directory The main directory on a disk. All other directories grow out of the root.

scanner A device you use to input printed information into the PC. The larger scanners work like photocopy machines. You use the smaller, handheld scanners by dragging the scanner over the material you want to scan.

SCSI An acronym for Small Computer System Interface. (You pronounce it "skuzzy.") SCSI is a standard for connecting some devices to a PC.

serial port A type of port on the system unit for attaching serial devices such as printers, modems, and other computers.

server See *file server.*

shell An interface between the operating system and the user.

shortcuts A feature of Windows 95 designed to enable you to quickly access other common or useful features. Shortcuts enable you to access a feature or file by clicking an icon on the desktop.

SIMM An acronym for single in-line memory module, which is a standardized circuit board that contains one or more RAM chips.

site A location of computer equipment and information. Often refers to the location of specific information on the Internet or World Wide Web.

software Programs comprised of coded instructions that you run on the computer to tell the hardware how to process information. Two basic types of software exist: system software and application software.

software suite   A collection of integrated software programs, such as Microsoft Office or Lotus SmartSuite.

sound board (or **sound card**)   An expansion board that enables your PC to produce music and other sounds. You usually use sound boards with multimedia applications.

spreadsheet   An application you use to manipulate numbers and perform calculations.

Start button   The button on the Windows 95 Taskbar that opens the Start menu from which you can start programs, get help, find files, change settings, or shut down Windows 95.

startup disk   See *system disk*.

storage device   A hardware device the PC uses to store data. For example, hard disks, floppy disks, and tapes are storage devices.

subdirectory   A directory that you create within another directory. Technically speaking, all directories on a disk are subdirectories of the root.

Super VGA (SVGA)   A high-quality video adapter standard.

surge suppressor   A power-protection device that filters the voltage between an outlet and a hardware component to prevent damage from sudden voltage changes.

syntax   The format and rules you use to issue a command, such as a DOS command.

system bus   The electronic wiring and adapter slots that enable the CPU to communicate with the RAM and peripheral devices.

system disk   A disk that has the operating system files on it so you can use it to start the computer.

system software   Software that instructs the different pieces of hardware how to operate and how to respond to your commands. For example, an operating system is a system software program.

Taskbar   A line near the bottom of the Windows 95 desktop where the Start button is located. Also, buttons on the Taskbar represent all programs that are currently running.

telecommunications   Using modems to exchange data between computers over phone lines.

uninterruptible power supply (UPS)   A power protection device that has a built-in battery to protect the computer components from a power outage.

UNIX   A 32-bit operating system often used on workstations and powerful personal computers. Originally, you had to know UNIX to be able to access the Internet.

user interface   A point of communication between the user and the PC. The DOS prompt and Microsoft Windows are examples of user interfaces.

video adapter   The circuit that controls the monitor. The video adapter is built into the motherboard or installed as an expansion card. The monitor connects to the video adapter via the video adapter port on the system unit. Common types include CGA, EGA, VGA, and SVGA.

video graphics array (VGA)   A common video graphics adapter standard that provides high resolution for displaying images on a monitor.

virus   A software program that some computer programmers maliciously design to damage existing files, programs, and disks. BBSs and infected disks usually surreptitiously spread viruses to the PCs of unsuspecting owners.

WAN   An acronym for Wide Area Network, a network that connects computers over long distances.

warm boot   Restarting a computer without turning it off first. See also *cold boot*.

what-you-see-is-what-you-get   See *WYSIWYG*.

wild card   A character you use to represent other characters. For example, in DOS a question mark (?) represents any single character. An asterisk (*) represents any group of characters.

window   An area on-screen that some programs, such as Microsoft Windows, use to display information. Windows contain applications, icons, and documents.

wizard   A feature of many Microsoft application programs designed to automate common tasks.

word processor   An application you use for entering and manipulating text.

WordPad   A Windows 95 accessory program used for creating and editing word processing documents.

World Wide Web   A subnetwork of the Internet that provides access to Internet sites via home pages.

write-protection   The process you use to protect disk files from being overwritten with new data.

WYSIWYG   An acronym for "what-you-see-is-what-you-get," a term that describes software programs that display information on the monitor exactly as it prints on the page. You pronounce it "wizzywig."

Index

Symbols

/(DOS command switch), 157
3¹/₂-inch disks, 55
    buying, 56
    defined, 204
    handling, 56-57
5¹/₄-inch disks, 55
    buying, 56
    defined, 204
    handling, 56-57

A

accelerators, graphics, 211
access time, 204
accessories (Windows 95), 152, 204
acoustic modems, 204
adapter cards (video display), 75-76
    memory, 77
addresses, 204
America Online, 196, 204
Apple Macintosh series, 11
applets (Windows 95), 204
applications
    defined, 204
    see also software
ASCII (American Standard Code for Information Interchange), 204
AUTOEXEC.BAT files, 101
    backing up, 135-137
    defined, 204

B

background computing, 205
backing up files, 34-35
    AUTOEXEC.BAT files, 135-137
    defined, 205
batch files, 205

baud rates (modems), 86
    defined, 205
BBS (bulletin board service), 205
BIOS (Basic Input/Output System), 205
bits, 205
booting, 205
    see also startup
Borland Paradox, 188
BPS (bits per second), 205
Briefcase program (Windows 95), 205
browsers (World Wide Web), 205
bulletin board service (BBS), 205
buses, 64
    cables, 89
    defined, 205
    local, 213
    mouse, 71
    networks, 89
buying software, 179-180
    communications programs, 192-194
    database programs, 186-188
    desktop publishing programs, 191-192
    DOS vs. Windows, 180-181
    e-mail programs, 196
    educational programs, 201
    financial programs, 201
    games, 201
    graphics programs, 188-190
    multimedia programs, 200
    online services, 196, 198-199
    personal information managers, 201
    spreadsheet programs, 185-186
    suites, 181-182
    utilities, 201
    word processors, 183-185
bytes, 205

C

cables
    bus, 89
    installing, 26-27
    monitor, 74
cache memory, 50
caches, 206
capacity, disk, 53
    defined, 206
cards
    expansion, 41, 61, 64
    video display expansion cards, 75-77
cascading windows (Windows 95), 118
case-sensitivity (DOS commands), 156
CD-ROM drives, 16, 59-60, 81-82
    defined, 206
    speed, 59, 208, 215
    troubleshooting, 31
CD-ROMs, 59, 81
CD\ command (DOS), 173
central processing unit (CPU), 13, 41, 43
    defined, 206
    startup, 28-29
        troubleshooting, 29-30
CGA (Color Graphics Adapter), 76
CGA (Computer Graphics Array), 206
chips, 42
    defined, 206
    see also microprocessors
clicking mouse, 206
clients, 206
clip art, 189, 206
Clipboard (Windows), 109
    defined, 206
clones, 206

Index

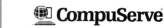

PLUG YOURSELF INTO...

THE MACMILLAN INFORMATION SUPERLIBRARY™

Free information and vast computer resources from the world's leading computer book publisher—online!

FIND THE BOOKS THAT ARE RIGHT FOR YOU!

A complete online catalog, plus sample chapters and tables of contents give you an in-depth look at *all* of our books, including hard-to-find titles. It's the best way to find the books you need!

- **STAY INFORMED** with the latest computer industry news through our online newsletter, press releases, and customized Information SuperLibrary Reports.

- **GET FAST ANSWERS** to your questions about Macmillan Computer Publishing books and software.

- **VISIT** our online bookstore for the latest information and editions!

- **COMMUNICATE** with our expert authors through e-mail and conferences.

- **DOWNLOAD SOFTWARE** from the immense Macmillan Computer Publishing library:
    - Source code and files from Macmillan Computer Publishing books
    - The best shareware, freeware, and demos

- **DISCOVER HOT SPOTS** on other parts of the Internet.

- **WIN BOOKS** in ongoing contests and giveaways!

TO PLUG INTO MCP: → **WORLD WIDE WEB: http://www.mcp.com**

FTP: ftp.mcp.com

The easy way to find answers

Easy Windows 95
ISBN: 1-56529-989-2
$19.99 USA
Pub Date 8/95

The *Easy* series is a full color, visual step-by-step tutorial covering over 100 common tasks and features. With screen shots for each step and a Document Gallery full of samples, this series is perfect for readers who prefer to learn visually.

Easy Excel for Windows 95
ISBN: 0-7897-0131-6
$19.99 USA
Pub Date 9/95

Easy Word for Windows 95
ISBN: 0-7897-0081-6
$19.99 USA
Pub Date 9/95

Easy PowerPoint for Windows 95
ISBN: 0-7897-0627-X
$19.99 USA
Pub Date 11/95

Complete and Return this Card
for a *FREE* Computer Book Catalog

Thank you for purchasing this book! You have purchased a superior computer book written expressly for your needs. To continue to provide the kind of up-to-date, pertinent coverage you've come to expect from us, we need to hear from you. Please take a minute to complete and return this self-addressed, postage-paid form. In return, we'll send you a free catalog of all our computer books on topics ranging from word processing to programming and the internet.

Mr. ☐   Mrs. ☐   Ms. ☐   Dr. ☐

Name (first) ☐☐☐☐☐☐☐☐☐☐☐ (M.I.) ☐ (last) ☐☐☐☐☐☐☐☐☐☐☐☐☐☐☐☐

Address ☐☐☐☐☐☐☐☐☐☐☐☐☐☐☐☐☐☐☐☐☐☐☐☐☐☐☐☐☐☐

☐☐☐☐☐☐☐☐☐☐☐☐☐☐☐☐☐☐☐☐☐☐☐☐☐☐☐☐☐☐

City ☐☐☐☐☐☐☐☐☐☐☐☐☐ State ☐☐ Zip ☐☐☐☐☐ ☐☐☐☐

Phone ☐☐☐ ☐☐☐ ☐☐☐☐ Fax ☐☐☐ ☐☐☐ ☐☐☐☐

Company Name ☐☐☐☐☐☐☐☐☐☐☐☐☐☐☐☐☐☐☐☐☐☐☐☐☐☐

E-mail address ☐☐☐☐☐☐☐☐☐☐☐☐☐☐☐☐☐☐☐☐☐☐☐☐☐☐

1. Please check at least (3) influencing factors for purchasing this book.

Front or back cover information on book ☐
Special approach to the content ☐
Completeness of content ☐
Author's reputation ☐
Publisher's reputation ☐
Book cover design or layout ☐
Index or table of contents of book ☐
Price of book ☐
Special effects, graphics, illustrations ☐
Other (Please specify): _____ ☐

2. How did you first learn about this book?

Saw in Macmillan Computer Publishing catalog ☐
Recommended by store personnel ☐
Saw the book on bookshelf at store ☐
Recommended by a friend ☐
Received advertisement in the mail ☐
Saw an advertisement in: _____ ☐
Read book review in: _____ ☐
Other (Please specify): _____ ☐

3. How many computer books have you purchased in the last six months?

This book only ☐   3 to 5 books ☐
2 books ☐   More than 5 ☐

4. Where did you purchase this book?

Bookstore ☐
Computer Store ☐
Consumer Electronics Store ☐
Department Store ☐
Office Club ☐
Warehouse Club ☐
Mail Order ☐
Direct from Publisher ☐
Internet site ☐
Other (Please specify): _____ ☐

5. How long have you been using a computer?

☐ Less than 6 months   ☐ 6 months to a year
☐ 1 to 3 years   ☐ More than 3 years

6. What is your level of experience with personal computers and with the subject of this book?

	With PCs	With subject of book
New	☐	☐
Casual	☐	☐
Accomplished	☐	☐
Expert	☐	☐

Source Code ISBN: 0-7897-0455-2

7. Which of the following best describes your job title?

Administrative Assistant .... ☐
Coordinator .... ☐
Manager/Supervisor .... ☐
Director .... ☐
Vice President .... ☐
President/CEO/COO .... ☐
Lawyer/Doctor/Medical Professional .... ☐
Teacher/Educator/Trainer .... ☐
Engineer/Technician .... ☐
Consultant .... ☐
Not employed/Student/Retired .... ☐
Other (Please specify): _____ ☐

8. Which of the following best describes the area of the company your job title falls under?

Accounting .... ☐
Engineering .... ☐
Manufacturing .... ☐
Operations .... ☐
Marketing .... ☐
Sales .... ☐
Other (Please specify): _____ ☐

9. What is your age?

Under 20 .... ☐
21-29 .... ☐
30-39 .... ☐
40-49 .... ☐
50-59 .... ☐
60-over .... ☐

10. Are you:

Male .... ☐
Female .... ☐

11. Which computer publications do you read regularly? (Please list)

_____
_____
_____
_____
_____
_____
_____
_____
_____

Comments:_____
_____
_____

Fold here and scotch-tape to mail.